Books by Louis H. Bean

The Art of Forecasting

The Graphic Method of Multiple Curvilinear Correlation

The 1964 Presidential Election Game

How to Predict the Stock Market

How to Predict Elections

The Art of Forecasting

THE RANDOM HOUSE SERIES IN FINANCE & INVESTMENT

EDITORS: Peter L. Bernstein & Gilbert E. Kaplan

The Art of Forecasting

Louis H. Bean

RANDOM HOUSE : NEW YORK

9 8 7 6 5 4 3 2

Copyright© 1969 by Louis H. Bean

All rights reserved under International and Pan-American
Copyright Conventions. Published in the United States
by Random House, Inc., New York, and simultaneously in Canada
by Random House of Canada Limited, Toronto.

Library of Congress Catalog Card Number: 74-85590

Manufactured in the United States of America

Typography & binding design
by Mary M. Ahern

FIRST PRINTING

FIK

CONTENTS

LIST OF CHARTS & TABLES

INTRODUCTION

Shortcuts to Forecasting

The main purpose of this book is to demonstrate that in much of the practice of forecasting in various fields, such as business activity, stock market fluctuations, voting behavior, and weather and crop fluctuations, you may do better with simple methods than with comprehensive or complex systems.

You may greatly simplify the job of forecasting if you consider forecasting as an art rather than a science. The art may lie in selecting and examining only one or two of the many series of data pertaining to a problem to serve as proxies or representatives of the others. The art may lie in identifying in the series to be predicted a relatively small number of significant turning point indications. The art may also consist of identifying certain repetitive patterns of fluctuations in a series of data in which historical repetition is theoretically a valid expectation. It is also part of the thesis of this book to show that only the simplest of tools for forecasting may suffice, for in many cases it is not necessary to mathematicalize, to compute equations or coefficients of regression and of simple and multiple correlation. Perhaps I should say that this does not indicate a prejudice against the modern computers, the wonderful labor-saving tools for economic and other forecasting model-builders, but where forecasting problems can be handled by simple approaches, and there are many such problems, the only tools required are a pencil, a supply of graph paper and, if you wish to splurge, an eraser. This is all the equipment used in the illustrations that form the body of this book.

The science of forecasting has reached the stage, thanks to the development of high-speed computers, where almost any number of factors and any amount of data can now be handled. But it has yet to be demonstrated that economic forecasting based on comprehensive models and many interrelated factors can predict when the next business depression will arrive, or how deep it will go; or what the stock market will do six months or a year from now; or, once the conventions have chosen their candidates, which of the nominees will be elected; or what the weather will be next year and what it will do to the farmers' crops. If you specify certain conditions that you assume will prevail in the future, the computer, on the basis of past relationships, will produce an answer, most expeditiously. But this is not forecasting. It is high-speed computing on the basis of specified assumptions. Change the assumptions and the computer will change the answer.

I have selected four topics to illustrate the general theme that the simple approach to forecasting can greatly simplify the job of the forecaster. These four topics are: (1) the business cycle, (2) the stock market, (3) presidential and congressional elections, and (4) weather and crops.

Interest in these topics stems from the fact that we are still a long way from being able to predict a year in advance, in spite of great activity and progress in the last twenty or thirty years. Lest this view seem exaggerated I suggest that you ask a group of economists where the level of business will be a year hence. You will find a third of them saying up, a third down and a third about the same or unchanged. Ask a group of stock market analysts where the stock market will be a year hence and most of them will guess it will not be much different from the present level. Ask a group of political scientists a year before an election who will win and you will obtain no common answer, for you will get lost in a discussion about probable candidates, issues and voter reaction, the business situation, the stock market and our military operations abroad, our race riots at home. Ask any weatherman about the amount of monthly rainfall or about the temperature twelve months away and he will tell you that he has trouble enough trying to figure out tomorrow's weather. Ask any crop reporting service about next year's yield per acre for any crop in any state or country, and you will be referred to the weatherman, who will advise you to assume normal weather and therefore a normal yield.

The simple approach to business cycle forecasting depends on the fact that the business cycle is the composite of many interrelated activities and that it represents the net effect of sequential processes that drive the economy as a whole so that activity in one industry implies dependent activity in another, concurrently or at some time later. For example, steel production may go up and down concurrently with automobile production, but the availability and cost of credit affects home building which later affects the demand for home appliances.

The scientific approach to forecasting the business cycle, which is usually represented by the Federal Reserve Board index of industrial production, a composite of more than two dozen industrial groups, would call for forecasting these individual components and adding up the individual forecasts. There is a simpler way. The U.S. Department of Commerce supplies a twenty-year monthly record of a large number of business indicators, some of them leading the fluctuations in the general business index, some moving concurrently with them, some changing later. From the leading series it is possible to select one or two that fairly consistently and logically fluctuate ahead of general business. From the group of concurrent series it is possible to select one or two that are proxies or the equivalent of the general business cycle.

Predicting the general course of the stock market as a whole can also involve you in a comprehensive scientific computer endeavor in which you would try to predict the level of the market six months or a year ahead by predicting each of some eighty component industrial groups, or to predict the effects of a dozen or twenty so-called technical indicators of the market. A moment's consideration will suggest what a task it would be to try to marshal all the necessary factors required to predict the course of the supply and demand affecting the costs, sales and profits of each of the component industry groups and, in addition, to predict the effects of domestic government policies and international developments and investor and speculator psychology.

This, of course, is not the way the practitioners of stock market forecasting go about their business. Because a truly scientific approach in depth is not practical, stock market forecasting on the part of some involves forecasting the general course of business and net corporate profits, while on the part of many others it involves trying to obtain clues as to the next move from the record itself. This drawing inferences as to the next move from the record itself is, of course, a form of necessary simplification and is in line with the theme of this book. However, my suggestions for recognizing when the market in general has attained a major or cyclical turning point represent the simplest in simplification. They merely call for identifying the course of an underlying trend and spotting the earliest indication of a change in that course. For anticipating the trend of the market over the next several years I suggest deriving it from projected gross national product and net asset values as proxies for guesses as to the level of corporate profits.

Predicting the most popular event in politics, the election of president and congressmen, also lends itself to the selective process for avoiding unnecessary comprehensive analyses. The basis for it is essentially the same as the basis for general economic forecasting. It depends upon the interrelationships among components of the national vote. The voting population of the United States is not homogeneous. There are geographic and community differences in economic status, occupations, ethnic origins, education, religious affiliation and political traditions. Despite these social and economic differences there is a good deal of similarity in the way voters respond to national issues and personalities; that is, in the shifts that take place from one election to the next. For example, the Democratic percentages in Virginia parallel those of Florida and Texas. You can use one as the proxy for the other two or for the South as a whole. In the same way you can use Ohio as proxy for Indiana, Illinois and a number of other states, and two or three of these combined as proxy for the nation as a whole. The availability of nationwide polls and polls in individual states makes it possible, as soon as the conventions have made their choices, to assess the electoral strength of each candidate, for a national poll can be translated directly into the party strength of individual states and, conversely, polls in individual states provide the basis for judging how the national vote may go. This, as already indicated, provides the basis for lining up the states for each candidate. The theme here is, as your state goes, so goes the nation and so goes your neighbor state. The national result in congressional elections takes its cue from the national presidential election, but in mid-term years there is a typical shift against the party in power, a definite case of a four-year historical repetition.

The three topics touched on so far, business cycle forecasting, stock market forecasting and election forecasting, present the choice between elaborate systems of forecasting and simple methods; the emphasis in this book is on the latter. This choice is possible because, for each area of forecasting, there is a plethora of interrelated data which may be coupled with generally accepted theories of economic and human behavior. But the fourth topic, long-range weather and crop predictions, allows no such choice. Ample data are available but the scientific knowledge concerning what causes year-to-year variations in weather is lacking. The annual variations in rainfall and temperature are generally considered to be as disorderly, as unpredictive, as the number of heads or tails in a series of tosses of a handful of pennies. The approach I suggest in this case is that randomness does not square with the fact that weather fluctuations are the end products of extra-terrestrial forces which we do not understand but which we know are features of an orderly extra-terrestrial system. With end products of universal order, there is reason to suspect some kind of orderliness or repetition. Can we find evidence of such repetitions useful for prediction?

At this point we need to recognize one other probability, namely, that the end products of an orderly system of nature may, in fact, be the results of combinations of cyclical forces for which we lack knowledge of their number, their amplitudes or their periodicities. We are not even certain that mathematicians can unscramble and reveal the original cyclical components. But we do know that combinations of cyclical components produce results that contain repeating patterns of variations that do not look at all like any of the individual original components. Our task in forecasting thus becomes one of searching the weather records for repeating patterns of fluctuations and of identifying the current pattern to be projected on the basis of historical counterparts. These historical repetitions may appear at fixed intervals or at regularly changing intervals and their duration may stretch over five, ten, fifteen or more years. The art called for in these cases consists of identifying these repeating patterns of fluctuations.

Crop yield variations, insofar as they are not the result of what man can do to affect yields, are obviously the results of many pre-season as well as growing-season weather factors. Their separate effects on yields are difficult to determine. In fact their effects may not be separate, but joint and complex. If it is recognized that the yield variations are, in fact, the end products of the numerous pre-harvest and growing-season weather variables, the yield variations may then be considered as the equivalent of the combined weather effects and, therefore, probably containing repeating patterns of fluctuations. Here, too, the task becomes nothing more than the search, by inspection, for repeating patterns and the identification of the current pattern in relation to the earlier ones. The real problem the forecaster has to face in making use of correspondences between a current segment of a record and earlier segments is reflected in the necessary qualification "if history continues to repeat itself." But this qualification is required for all forecasts, for every forecast is based on past relationships or past characteristics that are expected to hold for the forecast period. There is never a guarantee that new factors may not arise or that seemingly unimportant factors, not as yet taken into account in the analytical basis for forecasting, may not unexpectedly become important.

This does not mean that the practice of forecasting, whether by comprehensive or simple analysis, is not worthwhile. Far from it, as I hope the illustrations of the several simplified forms of forecasting in the following chapters will demonstrate.

Business Cycle Forecasting

PART I:

The centerpiece of this section on business cycle forecasting is the demonstration that from the mass of data now available a few business indicators may be selected that simply and adequately show the sequential order of the basic business cycle developments. From among those business indicators that lead the general course of business we can select the one dominant leading series as a general-purpose business cycle forecaster, namely, the measure of stock market prices. This measure may be considered as a proxy for the business and profit expectations of millions of investors, here and abroad. Since World War II, with one exception, its cyclical behavior has generally anticipated business cycle developments.

A more comprehensive view of business cycle developments and prospects may be obtained by selecting one or two series from those that lead, coincide with or follow the business cycle. One such selection, illustrated in Chapter 2, consists of five items, showing the impulses leading from interest rates to the stock market to new orders for durable goods to industrial production to capital expenditures and, finally, to the initial series of interest rates. A second combination is a simple demonstration of the interplay between interest rates, housing construction, consumer installment debt, and free reserves of the Federal Reserve Banks. Other sequential combinations are possible.

Another illustration, in Chapter 3, demonstrates a simple device for long-range projections of industrial production or G.N.P. required for maintaining high-level employment at specified levels of unemployment, for example at 4 per cent. The device is a simple graphic correlation in which the trend of production is revealed by production levels that have been associated with a given (4 per cent) level of unemployment since 1948.

The Business Cycle

CHAPTER 1

Business cycle forecasting has a very long history, but a very short one-word answer to the question, Can turns in the business cycle and the duration and magnitude of declines and recoveries be reliably predicted, say, a year in advance? The answer is no. Some can make fairly accurate guesses, based on assumptions concerning the possible consequences of key forces at work in the economy as a whole, but others, from the same set of facts, can produce reasonable-looking opposite views. Is this too bold a conclusion, doing inadequate justice to the technical, analytical and forecasting progress that has been made in recent decades and especially in recent years?

If the foregoing question is related to short-range forecasts of three or four months, a more favorable conclusion, as we shall see, is warranted. But even these efforts at short-term quantitative forecasting of the business cycle are still in the experimental stage. I refer particularly to forecasting either of the two most commonly used measures of the nation's business; one measure is the gross national product, or G.N.P. It represents all goods and services purchased by consumers and government agencies (local, state and federal), purchases by foreign countries in excess of their sales to us, and the increase or decrease in inventories. These several categories pretty well cover all the transactions that take place in our business world. When these are adjusted for price changes, we have, in effect, the sum total of all transactions in goods and services in physical terms, exclusive of the changes caused by price variations. The second measure of the nation's business represents directly the physical volume of goods produced. It is the total of the physical output of our factories, mines, farms and utilities; farm production being represented by food and textile manufactures.

The outstanding developments in business cycle forecasting over the past half century are:

1.   The extensive coverage and analysis of economic data by Dr. Wesley Mitchell, greatly expanded by the National Bureau of Economic Research. Much of this is now channeled into the official monthly publication of the Department of Commerce, *Business Conditions Digest.*

2.   The work of the Harvard Economic Committee during World War I and in the 1920's following sequences in the economic processes that make for business cycles and resulting in a business forecasting market letter which featured the Harvard A - B - C curves. The A curve represented speculation (stock prices) and tended to precede by several months the B curve which represented general business activity. The C curve, composed of money rates representing money supply and credit conditions, followed the B curve by several months. In passing, it may be noted that the correlations between these three indexes were more pronounced in the ten-year period 1903 - 13 of the original analysis than in the 1920's. This system of forecasting was abandoned in the early 1930's because of the abnormal divergence between the three curves during the late 1920's, when the A curve was lifted out of its normal course by the speculative boom of 1928 - 29, and the C curve was lowered abnormally by Federal Reserve policy. This is one of many instances in economic research where seemingly good statistical analyses for one period fail

4

or fall short of their promise when applied to conditions in a subsequent period.

3. The development of forecasting techniques by several government agencies, covering industrial, agricultural, monetary and fiscal activities, making use of multiple correlation (regression) analyses and trend projections, and stimulating similar research and forecasting interest in commerce and industry.

4. The development of a comprehensive system of presenting the national economy as the sum total of all production of goods and services, the gross national product, and the sum total of all income of individuals, the national income.

5. The advent of the electronic computer has made possible (*a*) the presentation of a large body of economic series by the Census Bureau of the Department of Commerce in its monthly bulletin *Business Conditions Digest,* grouped into three classes of leading, coincident and lagging economic indicators; and (*b*) the construction of economic models to determine the interrelationships among the many segments of the economy as a whole, in order to predict the course of business in general and, on the basis of past relationships, to estimate the possible future effect of various assumptions as to government or private action with regard to prices, wages, taxes, interest rates, profits, employment, foreign trade and practically any other important item in the economic model.

In this brief chapter, we are obviously unable to cover these current developments in detail. Ample literature is now available in books, journals and periodicals, including bibliographies, of past and current research on business cycle theory and forecasting practice related to the various segments and industries of the economy. I have chosen instead to touch on a few items that may be of interest to those who, not having research facilities, try to appraise current and future business conditions from the standard sources of information, such as the *Federal Reserve Bulletin* on finance and industrial production, the *Survey of Current Business* of the Department of Commerce, covering almost everything, and *Business Conditions Digest* of the Bureau of the Census.

One of these topics relates to the changing character of business cycles since World War II. Their amplitude of fluctuation has been reduced so greatly in recent years (1961-69) that some have raised the question, Is the business cycle dead? Another relates to the single economic series that since World War II has served as the best forecaster of the business cycle, namely, the stock market. The third topic has to do with the sequences among a few of the official business indicators selected and arranged to show coming changes in general production and employment, followed by changes in finance and capital investment. There follows a review of the accomplishments of the model builders and their limited success so far in forecasting the business cycle. The final topic, long-term trends, shows how one may very simply derive trends for an industry or for the economy as a whole for particular purposes, such as determining the volume of production required for full employment.

Is the Business Cycle Dead?

Business cycle optimists in the mid-1960's began to wonder whether the business cycle is dead. There seemed to be more statistical evidence for this view than is available for the theologians' argument that God is dead.

For more than two decades we had not had a major depression, the kind that characterized practically every decade prior to 1940, and particularly postwar decades. Moreover the minor cycles of these two decades had progressively diminished in amplitude and duration. From 1949 to 1954 we had a five-year cycle; from 1954 to 1958 a four-year cycle, from 1958 to 1961 a three-year cycle and, as I am inclined to read the record, from 1961 to 1963 a compressed two-year cycle, followed by a continuous expansion to 1969. The last cycle, that of 1961-63, had such a small amplitude in comparison with the wider swing of the 1958-61 cycle and the still wider swing of the one preceding that, that most students of business fluctuations considered the entire eight-year period from 1961 to 1969 a record experience in business expansion.

In further support of this optimistic view, the vast body of data now available yields a more meaningful understanding of the way our economy functions, how the various parts fit together, than we have ever had before. All of this has developed since the passage of the Employment Act of 1946, which placed upon the federal government the responsibility for shaping its fiscal and monetary policies so as to maintain an economic climate conducive to a maximum level of production, employment and purchasing power.

The role of the federal government has been stated many times and in many ways. In the 1967 Economic Report to the Congress the president stated it thus:

> . . . it is the continuing policy and responsibility of the Federal Government . . . with the assistance and cooperation of industry, agriculture, labor and state and local governments, to coordinate and utilize all its plans, functions and resources for the

purpose of creating and maintaining, in a manner calculated to foster and promote free competitive enterprise and the general welfare, . . . useful employment opportunities . . . for those able and willing and seeking to work, and to promote maximum employment, production and purchasing power.

This responsibility has been exercised with increasing seriousness. It has stimulated the interest of private and government organizations in conducting extensive research to find the growth trends in private and government spending, in production and sales, both in the aggregate and in the major groups engaged in manufacturing, construction, farming and private and government services—the growth trends that are necessary to sustain full employment. An example of this focusing on projections rather than on business cycle forecasts is the report "U.S. Economic Growth to 1975: Potentials and Problems," a Department of Commerce study prepared for the Joint Economic Committee of the Congress, and released in December 1966. It contains, in the words of the report, "the results of a year long study undertaken by the Congressional Joint Economic Committee staff to determine the most probable range of the potential economic growth of the U.S. Economy over the next decade and the problems that might be faced in achieving those objectives."

This study concentrates on changes in the nation's ability to produce goods, services and leisure and finds it has the potential for a rate of growth above the 3.5 per cent that prevailed between 1948 and 1965. It does not deal with the conventional concept of economic change or expansion from year to year. In other words, it does not deal with business cycle forecasting, which is our present concern, but points out the various combinations of government policies and programs that will be required if the long-range projection of full employment is to be attained and maintained.

There are a number of economic records that might be cited as evidence that since the Employment Act of 1946 we have grown in economic wisdom, with the result that the business cycle diminished in amplitude and duration between 1949 and 1961, and that the record expansion since early 1961 marked the beginning of the disappearance of the business cycle. One example is given in Chart 1. It shows four cycles

Chart 1.   Diminishing Cycles in Wages and Salaries in Mining, Manufacturing and Construction, 1948-1967

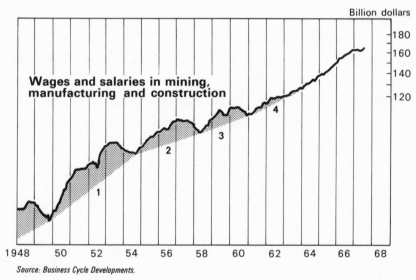

Billion dollars

Wages and salaries in mining, manufacturing and construction

Source: *Business Cycle Developments.*

in labor income in mining, manufacturing and construction between 1949 and 1963, followed by the steady prolonged expansion to the end of 1966. The first lasted nearly five years, the fourth only two years. The first by 1953 had risen substantially above its trend line, the fourth hardly at all. A chart

9

of industrial production or employment would show a similar decline in cyclical amplitude.

If this is evidence that the business cycle is dead, or if not dead, that it is about to disappear into a continuous trend of economic growth and sustained full employment, why talk about business cycle forecasting? The fact of the matter is that it will be many years before we will be able, either from the national viewpoint or from the viewpoint of our producing and employing industries, to lay aside the questions of next year's course of business and employment and how to anticipate both direction and magnitude of change.

This question of where the business cycle is at a given time, where it will be six months or a year or two later, is in fact the daily occupation of many people in the federal government and in the research offices of the major industries and corporations.

The Federal Reserve Board calibrates, measures and influences the blood stream of the economy, by influencing the flow of funds and the availability of credit, and records the course of industrial production in great detail. The Department of Commerce provides the current records for the nation as a whole and for each of the states of the volume of goods and services, of receipts and expenditures, generated by private and government activity. The Department of Labor and the Department of Commerce measure total and nonagricultural employment and unemployment. The Department of Commerce and the Securities and Exchange Commission supply current records and forecasts of business capital expenditures. The Department of Agriculture provides monthly and annual appraisals and forecasts affecting the wildly fluctuating farm commodity markets. And on top of all this there is the hawklike preoccupation of the Bureau of the Census with practically all the indicators of the business cycle, developments showing which lead the general course of business and which lag, or follow, and what per cent go up or down from month to month. These indicators are now watched, studied and interpreted closely in government and in the business community.

In view of all this proliferation of economic data, and of long-range projections and business cycle analyses, one would think that the course of the business cycle over the next six or twelve months would be clear, certainly clear to the workers in the business cycle vineyard. If the business cycle is not dead, certainly we ought to be able to predict what it will do during the coming six or twelve months, whether it will remain unchanged or go up or down, and by how much. Unfortunately our expanded knowledge of business cycle behavior does not yield this kind of quantitative, specific forecasting.

It is still prudent for men directing the affairs of business and government to have their feelers out for the possibility of a business decline following a period of prosperity. This is the reading of the long history of prosperity followed by depression or readjustment. It is the warning contained in the record of business cycle dates of peaks and troughs up to 1961, as the National Bureau of Economic Research has it, or up to 1963, as I am inclined to view the developments of the 1960's, for I think I see a trough in 1963 as well as 1961 that the National Bureau had not labeled as such as late as mid-1969.

The record, according to the tabulation of the National Bureau, shows 22 peace-time business expansions since 1854, with an average duration of 26 months. The 14 expansions prior to 1919 lasted, on the average, 25 months. The 8 since 1919 lasted, on the average, 28 months. There were:

   5 expansions of 10 to 19 months' duration
10 expansions of 20 to 29 months' duration
   6 expansions of 30 to 37 months' duration
   1 expansion of 50 months' duration

The 50-month expansion covers the period of the New Deal recovery from March 1933 to May 1937. There is some ground for considering one 12-month expansion from July 1932 to July 1933 and another of 32 months from September 1934 to May 1937. This would yield 23 expansions, 6 of 10 - 19 months, 10 of 20 - 29 months and 7 of 30 - 37 months.

By mid-1969 the expansion period following 1960 had already lasted over 100 months, about four times the average peace-time experience and twice the longest expansion.

Whether this latest expansion is measured from February 1961 or from a later date in 1963, it is necessary to recognize that military expenditures for the Vietnam War call for comparing the latest business cycle with the 1949 - 53 expansion of 45 months that included the period of the Korean War. This 45-month span exceeded peace-time expansion experience. The expansion from February 1961 to June 1969 had already exceeded the Korean War expansion by 55 months, or 60 per cent.

The record in Chart 1 is essentially a prolongation of the stable trend from 1961 to 1967. Other general measures of business fluctuations, such as the Federal Reserve index of industrial production, show only a slight decline in early 1967 followed by a resumption of the 1961 - 67 trend, though at a somewhat reduced rate of growth. But by mid-1969 inter-

12

est rates had been allowed to reach unprecedented high levels, prices were advancing faster than at any time since the Korean inflation of 1950-51, and warnings of a post-inflation recession or depression became more frequent. At this juncture it was quite unrealistic to assume that there would be no post-Vietnam letdown in industrial production and employment, even though it was not possible to discern when the peak would occur or how much of a business decline would follow it.

The record of reference dates provided by the National Bureau of Economic Research, showing when business cycle peaks and troughs have occurred and the duration from peak to trough as well as from trough to peak, contains an unusual feature not generally observed that pointed to the fiscal years 1966-67 and 1969-70 as the most likely periods for the appearance of the cycle peaks.

With twenty-six peaks in the hundred and twelve years since 1857 you would expect to find, on the average, two or three peaks in each decade just as a matter of chance distribution, and this is what actually shows up in the accompanying table. Here the reference dates are arranged by decades, beginning with the fiscal year 1856 (year beginning August). Note that except for three of these eleven decades, each shows two or three cycle peaks. This is the number per decade that you would normally get in a distribution of peaks of cycles having a total duration from peak to peak of about three years.

If you now ask in which year of each decade do business cycle peaks appear, the answer is not that you are just as likely to find a peak in any one of the ten years of the decade as in another. Of the twenty-six peaks shown in the table, note that twenty of them occur bunched in only four of the ten

13

years of a decade. Thus the fiscal year 7-8 has not had any peak in all the eleven decades. The fiscal years 0-1, 1-2, 3-4 and 5-6 have had only one peak each, and the year 4-5 only

Table 1. *Reference Years of Business Cycle Peaks and Duration of Subsequent Contraction (Months)* *(year beginning August)*

Year in decades	0-1	1-2	2-3	3-4	4-5	5-6	6-7	7-8	8-9	9-0	Total
Decade:											
1850-1859							18				1
1860-1869	8			32					18		3
1870-1879			65								1
1880-1889		38					13			10	3
1890-1899			17		18					18	3
1900-1909			23				13			24	3
1910-1919			23						7	18	3
1920-1929			14				13		18		3
1930-1939							13				1
1940-1949					8				11		2
1950-1959						13	9			9	3
1960-1969											
	1	1	5	1	2	1	6	0	4	5	26

Table 2. *Reference Years of Business Cycle Troughs and Duration of Subsequent Expansion (Months)* *(year beginning August)*

Year in decades	0-1	1-2	2-3	3-4	4-5	5-6	6-7	7-8	8-9	9-0	Total
Decade:											
1850-1859					30				22		2
1860-1869	46							18			2
1870-1879	34								36		2
1880-1889					22			27			2
1890-1899	20			18			24				3
1900-1909	21				33			19			3
1910-1919		12			44				10		3
1920-1929	22			27				21			3
1930-1939		50						80			2
1940-1949						37				45	2
1950-1959					35			25			2
1960-1969											
	5	2		2	5	1	1	6	3	1	26

14

two. But the year 8-9 has had four peaks, 9-0 has had five peaks, 2-3 has had five peaks, and 6-7 has had six peaks. While this again reflects the predominance of cycles of three to four years' duration, it is nevertheless striking to find twice the concentration of peaks in the year 6-7 (corresponding to 1966-67) than one would normally expect. This did not mean, of course, that the 1961-66 business expansion had by February 1967 already terminated, but it did argue for, and served to justify, the president's directive to his executive departments to exercise their responsibility in cooperation with business, labor and agriculture to help maintain the economy on an even keel. For a variety of reasons, including military expenditures and tax and interest rate policies, a 1966-67 recession of only minor proportions materialized.

Since our focus is on business cycle forecasting, the implication that a business cycle peak was "destined" to show up in 1966-67 suggested the next question: Suppose history were to repeat and the 1961-67 expansion were to terminate in 1966-67, could one have drawn any conclusion regarding how long the following contraction would last? Periods of contraction have ranged between the extremes of eight months and sixty-five months, but most of them have lasted either about a year (thirteen months) or about a year and a half (eighteen months).

Again the year 6-7 presented a prophetic peculiarity. Of the six peaks that have occurred in the sixth year of each decade, one was followed by a contraction of only nine months, one of eighteen months, while the other four lasted thirteen months. Did that mean that, given a recession in 1967, the best guess that could have been made in February 1967, without benefit of an examination of what was actually taking place within the structure of the economy (such as the down-

15

ward course of new orders, the decline of automobile production, countered by an upturn in residential construction, and more ample loan funds and increased military expenditures), was that it might last only about a year and therefore recovery could be expected to set in sometime before the end of 1967?

This general reading of the past was later corroborated.

Following these records of business cycle peaks and contractions, we note a better than fifty-fifty chance of a business letdown for the year 9-0, or 1969-70. There have been five recessions in the year 9-0 in the eight decades since 1880. By mid-1969 this hint began to take on the appearance of reality in view of the growing concern over inflation, high interest rates, and evidences of slowdown in various industries, including a decline in the stock market.

The Sequential Order in Business Cycle Developments

CHAPTER 2

Business cycle forecasters have always hoped to find certain causal factors that produce the cyclical variations in industrial activity, employment and purchasing power. These causal factors have been looked for in sun-spot cycles, in innovations, in financial operation, in corporate appropriations for capital investment, in consumer attitudes and expected spending, and other disturbances. The sequential order in business cycle developments, insofar as it prevails, is today basic in forecasting efforts, whether forecasting for a single industry, like steel or housing construction; for components of the gross national product, such as inventory changes; or for the total gross national product.

From the economic data now generally available we can draw several illustrations of the utility and limitations of searching for forerunners of general business activity. First, there is the problem of finding a single forecaster of the business cycle as measured by the cycles in industrial production, and second, the problem of recognizing the sequential processes in business cycle developments, using only a selected few of the many indicators.

The Stock Market As a Prime Forerunner of the Business Cycle

It is generally accepted that the best measure of the trend of the physical volume of general business is the Federal Re-

17

serve Board index of industrial production, and that its cyclical changes are our best measure of the business cycle. This index correlates highly with all the other central economic measures, such as total employment and unemployment, the money income of consumers, and corporate profits. Its cyclical turning points, the dates when business activity in general reaches its peaks and troughs, are practically identical with the dates of the business cycle peaks and troughs as selected by the National Bureau of Economic Research for official and general use.

Is there also a single best forerunner of the business cycle, the one best leading economic indicator? If you search among the list of official leading or forecasting business indicators for the best of the lot, you invariably come up with the index of industrial stock prices. The general similarity between the cyclical changes in industrial stock prices and those of industrial production is striking, even though, as can be seen in Chart 2, there are discrepancies as well.

In this illustration I have emphasized the cyclical movements in both indexes by connecting their low points and shading the areas above the connecting lines.

For the entire twenty-year period 1948 - 67 there is general cyclical correspondence and general consistency in the sequential relation between the comparable high points as well as between the comparable low points. Each low point in industrial stock prices is followed some months later by low points in the industrial production index. This lag is not fixed. It varies roughly between six months to nearly a year. Note for example that the stock price peak of January 1966 was followed eleven months later by a peak in industrial activity in December 1966, and that the stock market low of October 1966 was followed nine months later by a low in industrial activity.

There is also a fair degree of similarity between the amplitudes of the two sets of cyclical changes. Exact correspondence would be surprising in view of the fact that one is a measure of price changes and the other a measure of physical pro-

Chart 2. Stock Price Cycles as Forerunners of Industrial Production Cycles, 1948-1967

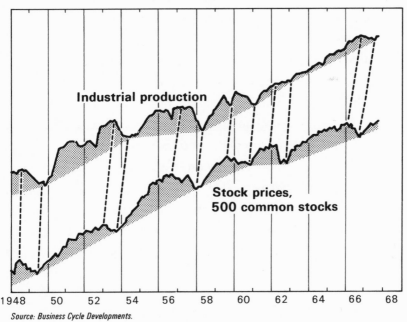

Source: *Business Cycle Developments.*

duction. But this general similarity in amplitude does not hold for the 1962 and the 1966 sharp declines in the stock market index. For an explanation of the 1962 exception, it is necessary to review first the high degree of speculation reached in the winter months of 1961-62 and then the controversy between President Kennedy and the spokesman of the steel industry when the latter proposed steel price increases. This controversy raised fears about price and profit prospects not only in the steel industry but in industry in general, and undoubtedly helped accentuate the decline in the stock market. On the other hand, to understand the failure of industrial activity to decline in conformity with the decline in the stock market, it is necessary to note the tax and other policies the Kennedy Administration adopted to prevent an expected recession in 1962-63 and to stimulate a faster rate of growth for the economy as a whole in order to lower the prevailing rate of unemployment.

Similarly, for an explanation of the failure of industrial production to decline more than it did in 1966-67 in conformity with the sharp decline in stock prices in 1966, it is necessary to examine the various interpretations placed by government and private economists and government and business officials on the probable economic impact of our expensive involvement in Vietnam. The increase in military expenditures and the availability of funds for commerce and industry in spite of high interest rates will be found to have sustained the 1967-1969 relatively high level of industrial production, employment and consumer income, following the 1966 stock market decline.

That this sequential relationship between stock prices and business cycles has prevailed during the twenty-five years since World War II does not necessarily mean that it will hold true at all times in the future. The checkered history of this relationship must always be kept in mind. It held true for many years before World War I and for a good part of the 1920's. It apparently does not hold true in periods of more than normal economic uncertainties, such as those that prevailed during World Wars I and II, and during our greatest

20

industrial depression of the 1930's. In the midst of such unusual times, most unusual uncertainties dominate and the normally wise can see the future no more clearly than the rest.

The Sequential Order Among Business Cycle Indicators

The widely used business indicators of today are, in my view, a monument of credit to the Harvard A-B-C curves of the 1920's. Following Mitchell's probing into the statistical evidence of the processes by which booms developed into crises, then into depression and then into revival and another boom, the grouping of the statistical series into three sequential groups was a logical step. The same logic pervades business cycle analysis today in the form of "leading," "coincident" and "lagging" indicators. Hundreds of different economic records have been calibrated according to their high points and low points, the duration between these points, the amplitude of their movements and the timing of these points in relation to the accepted dates of the peaks and troughs of the general business cycle.

The most recent development in the search for leading or predictive indicators is the development of measures of diffusion. Where an economic series, like the Federal Reserve Board index of industrial production, is the aggregate of a large number of component series that do not all move in the same direction or at the same time, it is of interest to tabulate how many, at any time, are advancing. Many of these broadly based series have now been so analyzed and the results presented as diffusion indexes.

The charts and tables, available monthly in the Bureau of the Census bulletin *Business Conditions Digest,* present

21

the postwar record for a substantial number of leading indicators, roughly coincident indicators, lagging indicators and "other selected U.S. series." These series presumably are the most useful and meaningful for judging where the economy is and in which direction it is going. Each of these records is charted from 1948 to date, and, for a selected number, the percentages of components rising, from month to month and over a nine-year span, are also shown, these being the diffusion indexes.

Each of the three groups of indicators—leading, coincident and lagging—grouped according to cyclical timing, are also classified according to economic processes that are listed as:

1. Employment and unemployment (14 series)
2. Production, income consumption and trade (8 series)
3. Fixed capital investment (14 series)
4. Inventories and inventory investment (9 series)
5. Prices, costs and profits (11 series)
6. Money and credit (17 series)

There are two additional classifications, foreign trade and payments (6 series) and federal government activities (9 series), but these "other selected series" are not classified according to cyclical timing.

As forecasting tools, how good are these leading indicators and the changes taking place within each of them? An examination of the charts of leading indicators and those showing their transformation into diffusion indexes reveals why we are not yet at the point in business cycle forecasting that permits a reliable quantitative statement concerning where the general level of business, or any of its segments, will be six months or a year later. For example, the fact that the leading indicators showed downward trends during 1966, not unlike their behavior in 1962, could not with certainty be construed as forecasting an impending decline in general business and employment, for the 1962 experience was not followed by a business recession.

Furthermore, most of the leading indicators, either in original form or as diffusion indexes, show great irregularities from month to month. There are no stable relations between the peak-trough intervals among the leading indicators and the peak-trough intervals in the indexes of general business.

Table 3.   Classification of Leading Indicators by Relative Length of Lead at Peaks

Long Leads median lead (months)		Short Leads median lead (months)	
Unit Labor Costs	27	Price-Labor Cost Ratio	6
Hiring rate	10	Help Wanted Advertising	4
Lay-off rate	9	Non-farm placements	5
Change, unfilled orders, durable goods	24	Unemployment rate	3
Vendor performance	27	Average work week	7
Inventory investment	22	New orders, durable goods	6
Buying policy, production materials	19	Contracts for plant and equipment	5
Prices, industrial raw materials	6	Common stock prices	4
Housing permits	14		
Net new businesses	16		

The lack of uniformity in the number of months between turning points in leading indicators and in general business is obviously a major problem in business cycle forecasting. This implies that we are a long way from the happy day when a group of business analysts and forecasters will be able to arrive at a unanimous judgment as to where we are in a business cycle development with sufficient certainty to serve as a firm policy guide. An analysis by Edgar R. Fiedler of Bankers Trust Co. (in the 1962 Proceedings of the Business and

Economics Section of the American Statistical Association) supports this point. He classified leading indicators into two groups, as shown in Table 3.

Not only is there the wide range of leads among these indicators (from averages of 4 to averages of 27 months) but not one of these indicators shows a consistently uniform or fixed lead. Take the 27-month-long lead of unit labor costs. Going back to 1920, Fiedler shows the median to consist of leads of 7, 13, 46, 27 and 12 months. The median 6-month short lead of the price-labor cost ratio is based on leads of 11, 10, 1, 2, 6, 29, 4, 12, and in one instance (1920) it did not lead, but lagged one month. In the case of the short lead of new orders for durable goods, since 1923 the leads have been 4, 11, 5, 5, 6, 8, 11, and in one case (1929) there was no specific cycle. The average long lead of housing permits is derived from leads ranging between 3 and 29 months.

It is not at all surprising that the business analyst or forecaster, browsing through the many indicators that the National Bureau has selected as the most useful, finds the evidence on the status of the business cycle confusing, is uncertain about when to expect a peak or trough or how high a peak and how low a trough he should expect.

Undoubtedly other forms of presentation of these indicators are now being developed in the interest of greater predictability and simplicity. There is certainly need for some official aggregation of these many indexes into a few simple ones. As the indexes stand, they require considerable time and effort if one is interested in discerning the sequences that are developing within the economy and the point at which an important change in direction may be taking place.

But even if analysis could be facilitated by aggregating these indicators to provide clearer impressions of central tendencies, certainty as to when to expect a peak or trough would still be lacking. Geoffrey Moore and Julius Shiskin in *New Indicators of Business Expansions and Contractions* show the results of combining twelve leading indicators, five co-incident indicators and six lagging indicators. These are now shown monthly in the *Business Conditions Digest* of the Bureau of the Census. The composite of the twelve leading indicators, as I read the record, reached a peak about 30 months ahead of the 1953 business peak, about 18 months ahead of the 1955 peak, and about 12 months ahead of the 1959 peak. Fiscal and monetary policy-makers need more uniform timing than this.

Diffusion indexes present similar and additional analytical difficulties and tribulations.

The limitations as well as possible uses of these indicators are recognized by Geoffrey Moore of the National Bureau in his book *Business Cycle Indicators* as follows:

Taken together, the various current indexes illustrate an important principle. Individual index numbers are fallible, but they are also, to a degree, consilient. Diffusion indexes are no exception. Consequently it is well to be guided by a number of them rather than by any single one. Armed with a workable set of diffusion indexes covering different economic sectors and utilizing various techniques, the analyst may eventually be able to make judgments on the scope of current movements that will not only stand the test of history but actually assist him in his appraisal of future prospects. This assistance, I may add, may not come in the form of specific economic aggregates on specific future dates. It may merely serve to confirm or to modify some judgments or assumptions that he had already formulated on the basis of other information. Or it may be helpful only when there is an extended period of uncertainty as to the direction of business trends. There is room for many contributions of these varied kinds to the problem of business forecasting and my guess is that students of diffusion indexes will make their share of them as we learn more about how to construct and interpret them. Although they may not enable us to take the whole measure of the business cycle, it is challenging, at least, to have another dimension to work with.

For the general follower of the business cycle not interested in the behavior and significance of a hundred different indicators, whether in actual numbers or in the form of diffusion indicators, there are only a few series that need to be watched. This minimum number is sufficient to provide a sequential view of the processes within the totality of business. This sequential view differs somewhat from the view of business developments presented in the Census Bureau's six groupings of employment, production, investment, inventories, prices-costs-profits, and money and credit. It starts with a recognizable causal fact at a crucial point in the business cycle and traces its impact sequentially.

A crucial point can be, for example, a money supply crisis that develops at the peak of a business cycle and sets off a fairly obvious chain of developments. A tight money situation is reflected in high interest rates and in a decline in stock prices as the "speculation industry" anticipates or sees a decline in new orders for durable goods and in construction. These developments are followed by a decline in industrial production, employment, wages, sales and profits, consumer installment purchases and expenditures for new plant and equipment. As this chain of consequences takes place the speculation industry notes the easing in the money supply and in credit reflected in lower interest rates which it interprets as a sign of impending recovery warranting the anticipation of improved earnings and higher stock prices. The

26

lowered interest rates stimulate the construction industry and new orders, recovery in industrial production and profits, increased demand for labor, for additional inventories, for more plant capacity and equipment, increased demand for credit by industry and by consumers buying on installment—all leading to competition for and the full use of loanable funds and again to high interest rates. This is an oversimplified view of the sequential processes that produce business contractions followed by expansions, but it is in line with what a limited selection of business indicators clearly shows for the period since World War II.

An illustration of the sequential view is contained in Chart 3, which is to be read from bottom to top. It starts with a series of interest rates and is followed by four other series in this order—stock prices, new orders for durable goods, industrial production, expenditures for new plant and equipment—and these are topped by the interest-rate series we started with. In this array interest rates are initially viewed as representing stimulating money and credit conditions, and finally viewed as representing depressing money and credit conditions. In other words, the business cycle processes start with money and end with money.

Of course, there is really no fixed starting point in the continuing industrial process, because at every point in time prevailing conditions are the results of previous events and these results in turn bring on subsequent events. But there are crucial points where a few factors dominate in altering a situation from one of expansion to contraction or contraction to expansion.

If, then, we recognize (in Chart 3) that 1948, 1953, 1957, 1959 and 1966 were crucial points at business peaks producing substantially higher interest rates than those prevailing

27

at their preceding troughs, there is revealed an interesting series of sequences. These sequences are indicated by the slanting lines which are drawn to connect the low points and also

Chart 3.   The Sequential Order Among Five Selected Business Cycle Indicators, 1948-1967

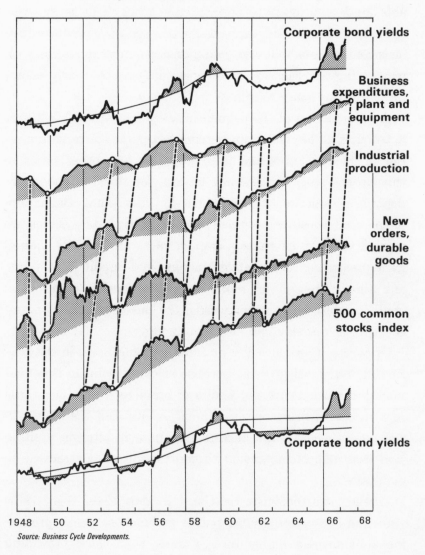

Source: *Business Cycle Developments.*

28

the high points of two of the series, namely stock prices and expenditures for plant and equipment, stock prices being the prime series among the leading indicators and expenditures for plant and equipment being the prime series among the lagging indicators.

In addition to the vertically slanting connecting lines, two other graphic devices need to be noted. With the exception of the interest-rate series and following the device used in Chart 2, there are trend lines connecting the low points of each series and the areas above these lines are shaded. The purpose here too is to reveal the cyclical movements more clearly exclusive of trend. In the case of interest rates shown at the bottom of the chart there are two trends. The purpose here is to note the relatively high level of interest rates associated with the end of business expansions, and the relatively low rates prevailing during periods of expansion. Just as the other series show expansions and contractions taking place in relation to their trends, so interest rates have been relatively high or low in relation to the interest-rate trend. For example, in 1953 interest rates marked the retarding effects of money and credit when they exceeded 3.5 per cent. In 1959 they marked the retarding effect of money and credit when they exceeded 5 per cent. Similarly, interest rates below 3 per cent were associated with the 1954 recovery but the recovery period of 1963-65 developed with interest rates only slightly below 4.5 per cent.

We are now in a position to note the sequences that are sandwiched in between the interest-rate series at the bottom and top of Chart 3. The sequences or lags developed after 1950. In 1948-49 the lag between the leading indicator, stock prices, and the lagging indicator, expenditures for plant and equipment, was relatively short. Another exception shows up in 1966. The high point in interest rates coincides with the low point in stock prices, contrary to previous experiences showing a lag. The explanation may perhaps be found in the fact that this interest-rate series does not adequately portray the money and credit conditions of late 1966, when government action was taken outside the commercial banking field to provide funds for certain projects below the prevailing high rates.

The lag between stock prices and expenditures for plant and equipment provides a fairly good measure of the time involved between the initial and final stages of the expansion and contraction processes. It is neither as long nor as fixed a period as one would expect. In the 1953-56 expansion the lag between the best leader, stock prices, and plant and equipment expenditures, the best lagging series, was about a year, but this was reduced to about six months in the 1959-62 period, and apparently to not much more than six months since 1962. It is also evident that the periods of expansion and contraction are not the same, that the stock market fairly well anticipates the duration of both expansions and contractions and that money and credit conditions shape the course of expansions and contractions. A prolonged period of relatively low interest rates like that of 1962-65 means a prolonged period of expansion, and a short period of low interest rates, as in 1958, means a short expansion period.

There are other sequences that can be developed from the eighty-eight selected economic indicators. Here we have merely shown the lags between five important points in the business cycle process in banking, speculation, advance orders, production and capital expenditures. But there are sequential lags among interest rates, housing construction, consumer installment debt, changes in business inventories and free reserves of the central banks; among the various measures of employment and hours worked per week; among production, labor costs, profits, appropriations and expenditures for plant expansion. There are also lags among purchases of raw materials, production, sales, inventories and borrowings.

One of these combinations—the sequences among interest rates, building permits, consumer installment debt and free reserves of the Federal Reserve Banks—is shown in Chart 4. To emphasize the relation of interest rates to these three demands for money and credit I have drawn a trend line connecting the high points in the interest-rate series, and trend lines in the other series connecting their low points, with departures from the trend lines shaded.

The inverse relation between interest rates and private housing permits is immediately obvious. There is a noticeable lag throughout, except in 1966. Consumer installment debt is also related inversely to interest rates with a somewhat longer lag than housing permits; the same holds for changes in business inventories.

The series of free reserves, which tops this array, shows, with inverted scale, whether member banks of the Federal Reserve System have overborrowed or not, and therefore the reason for the relatively high or low interest rates. When the rate of borrowing uses up free reserves, it becomes a clear sign that recovery is about to slow down and turn into contraction.

Toward the end of 1966, the shortage of reserves and high interest rates had greatly reduced home building. But as borrowing was restricted, reserves increased and interest rates declined, new building permits improved. These adjustments came about without the usual lags.

31

The sequential view of business expansions and contractions in Chart 3 throws some light on the anomaly of 1962, when a sharp decline in stock prices had no apparent justi-

Chart 4.   Relation of Interest Rates to Cycles in Housing, Consumer Installment Credit and Free Reserves

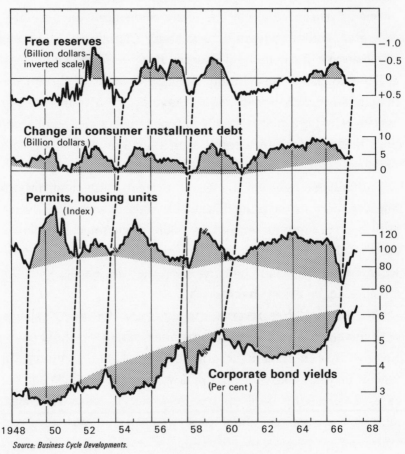

Source: Business Cycle Developments.

fication in money, credit and business conditions. It is usually assumed that this decline in stock prices was not prophetic as in the past, but the sequential view shows a minor cyclical development during 1962-63, which was presumably checked by the tax measures proposed by the Kennedy Administration to stimulate capital expansion in order to cut down the unemployment rate, to stimulate the growth rate and to guard against a recession following the stock market decline. Government apparently interfered with stock market prophecy.

This form of analysis shows that we experienced the beginning of a business cycle advance after January 1963, not February 1961 as generally thought. But whether this expansion began in 1961 or 1963, we faced in 1966-67 the same quandary faced by the Harvard economists at the end of 1928 when they perceived evidences of a business downturn but could not see it in their stock market curve A. They could not distinguish between the cyclical element and the steep trend element. Similarly the 1963-67 trend element in general business was not clearly discernible by the end of 1967. If the advance of 1963-67 was considered partly cyclical and partly trend, how much was contributed by the trend and how much by the cycle could not be obvious unless a slowdown or a decline in industrial activity developed during 1967 and until the next advance began.

The beginning of 1967 brought accumulating evidence among the indicators of a possible decline in general business activity, but, as usual, no basis for predicting that a downturn was inevitable, especially in view of official concern and of the supporting force of government spending for military purposes. Nevertheless it was appropriate to inquire how long a 1967 recession would last if it did develop. The clue lay in the nine-month span between the 1966 peak and bottom of the stock market index. It suggested that a 1967 recession might not last as long as a year, and it didn't.

This was as far as business cycle analysis and forecasting could take us. We were then at the point usually reached in all forecasting efforts where the record of the past and a clear

33

view of current trends called for a forecast to be followed by the qualification "if history repeats."

It is becoming quite clear that the real function of economic indicators is not prediction but prevention. This could not have been said in the 1920's, for there were lacking the responsibility and the means for prevention. The only agency then in existence with responsibility and some power was the Federal Reserve Board. It was charged then, and still is, with responsibility over bank loans and interest rates to help keep the commodity price level and the course of business activity stable. The federal government, whose purchases of goods and services then amounted to no more than 3 per cent of the national total of goods and services, could do little more than to exercise its power of persuasion on key business leaders, a practically ineffective means for preventing inflation and recession.

Today the federal government not only has the responsibility, as already indicated, but a great deal of economic power, for in addition to the use of monetary means to influence capital investment and the course of business and employment it can affect directly the level of economic activity, both through tax policy, which adds or subtracts from general purchasing power, and through changes in various federal expenditure programs. The federal government contributes about a fifth to the total national purchases of goods and services. Curtailment or expansion in government spending can retard or stimulate the economy, and business indicators play a very substantial role in discussions and arguments over what government policy should be when they point to inflation, as they appeared to do early in 1966, or to recession, as they seemed to do in late 1966.

Arriving at the right decision as to what action government should take when indicators point to the need for preventive

34

or stimulating measures is not simple. Economists and others do not interpret business indicators the same way, and even when there is agreement and action is clearly required, there may not be agreement among economists or legislators as to which policies to adopt.

Short-Range Forecasting of Gross National Product and Its Components

CHAPTER 3

Statisticians and economists in government and industry are engaged in forecasting the trends and cyclical movements in individual components of the nation's business activity, such as housing construction, the production of steel, automobiles, food and clothing. Many examples may be found in the economic journals and books on business economics and business forecasting, which describe methods, techniques and results. It is not the purpose here to cover the wide field of forecasting research in particular industries, but, rather, to note the progress that has been made in recent years in providing a comprehensive view or model of the U.S. economy in which the many different components are brought together in logical and mathematical relationships for the benefit of those engaged in national government policy-making decisions affecting the private as well as the government segments of the total economy.

The logic resorted to in forecasting the changes in the economy as a whole, measured in terms of the gross national product, is fairly simple. It consists of selecting the most important components of G.N.P., namely, personal consumption expenditures, private business capital investment, government purchases of goods and services, the net export of goods and services, and the net change in unsold goods, namely, inventories—and then devising ways of predicting these components, usually from a quarter to a year in advance.

To obtain estimates of consumption expenditures, for example, it is the practice to start with the gross national product, deduct capital consumption allowances (depreciation), add subsidies, deduct corporate profits and inventory changes, add (1) state employment insurance benefits, (2) business and other government transfer payments to individuals, (3) interest paid by government and by consumers and (4) dividends, and finally subtract personal tax and non-tax payments—and thus arrive at an estimate of disposable income of all individuals.

Some of these items are easy to predict or project; others are difficult. Most of them are interrelated and dependent on one another. This presents a difficult statistical analytical problem for it is necessary to assign the relative effects of these separate but interrelated items on the total G.N.P. or on a major component.

It has already been pointed out that there is a high degree of dependence and similarity between quarterly estimates of G.N.P. in physical constant-dollar terms and industrial production, and that the latter has a wider range of fluctuation. Model builders have concentrated more on figuring out how to predict G.N.P. variations rather than industrial production. The latter can be approximated once G.N.P. in constant dollars has been projected.

Recent progress in national economic model-building and forecasting has been reported in the *Survey of Current Business,* May 1966, by Liebenberg, Hirsh and Popkin, staff members of the Office of Business Economics. Louis Paradiso, assistant director of that office, discusses the problems in forecasting the most volatile of all G.N.P. segments, namely, inventory changes, in the book *How Business Economists Forecast,* edited by Butler and Kavesh.

High and low inventories and their changes, according to Paradiso, "have at times accentuated downturns or helped bolster recoveries from each of the four postwar recessions. Shifts in inventory investment have been important in determining the shape and duration of the business cycle." In view of the importance of this component it is worth noting as an example of analytical procedure the major steps involved in making a forecast of inventory changes.

"First it is necessary to appraise the quarterly pattern of demand for the major types of goods, business plant and equipment, and consumer goods. . . . The next large group to forecast is consumer goods . . . in three parts: (a) auto sales and output; (b) other consumer durables such as furniture, appliances, books; and (c) non-durable goods with particular emphasis on apparel. . . . The next step is to evaluate the prospects for price changes. . . . The next phase in arriving at an inventory forecast is to examine the recent trends of inventory sales ratios for major groups of manufacturing industries and of trade lines. . . . In estimating inventory change through use of inventory sales ratio, two forecasts must be made: (a) a projection of overall inventory-sales ratio, and (b) a projection of sales for industries considered. . . .

"Thus it becomes clear that this approach is far from mechanical. At every stop judgment is required. . . . On the whole, forecasts obtained by the approach generally have been reasonably good, although at times predictions have missed the mark by a wide margin and on some occasions even the turning points have not been correctly called."

Summarizing this and other procedures in forecasting short-term quarterly changes in inventories, Paradiso concludes: "Although the quantitative approach through the use of regression equations which express inventory investment in

terms of causative factors is promising, this should be regard-
ed as the starting point from which a final forecast is derived.
In the end, the forecast must encompass an appraisal of
a variety of factors and a consideration of businessmen's current inventory policies. Basic to a reliable forecast is a thorough knowledge of business developments in their major aspects and some detailed consideration of the inventory-sales
trends by major industries and commodities."

Not at all a simple analytical task.

Even if satisfactory forecasts of annual and quarterly forecasts of inventory changes were possible, they would still
present difficulties when used as one of the variables in forecasting the business cycle as measured by the gross national product or industrial production. In the first place, the inventory series is classified as one that generally lags *after*
the business cycle. Secondly, as is the case with many other
lagging and even leading indicators, there is no fixed stable
interval between the turning points in the inventory series
and in the business cycle. In 1949 the inventory series turned
up seven months *before* the business cycle trough; in 1954,
two months before. In 1958 and 1961, it turned up seven and
eight months *after* the troughs, and in 1967 three months
before.

Since technical, as contrasted with judgmental, business
cycle forecasting must depend heavily on economic series
that anticipate or lead, with stable time intervals, erratic shifts
in lag, as illustrated here in the case of inventories, and already referred to earlier in discussing the leading indicators,
make for errors in predicting gross national product by means
of economic models or other statistical relationships.

The Department of Commerce report on the progress in
developing its quarterly *Econometric Model of the United*

States (May 1966) makes this amply clear. The following facts and conclusions are drawn from that report.

The Department of Commerce model, capitalizing on the experience of other model-builders, consists of forty-nine equations, divided into six groups, which explain:

1. Components of G.N.P.
2. Prices and wage rates
3. Labor force and employment-related magnitudes
4. Income components
5. Monetary variables
6. Miscellaneous variables needed to round out the model

The Department of Commerce report describes the equations in these six categories "and points out the principal mechanisms that merge the different parts into an interdependent system."

For our purposes, the main interest lies in the results obtained by testing this model to see how it would have worked over short periods not exceeding a year, particularly in predicting turning points in the two periods of greatest cyclical changes since 1948, namely, 1953-54 and 1957-58. For the more recent years, the test may not be as significant since the economic variables have been marked by relatively stable trends.

The test covering the period 1953-61 consisted of three separate four-quarter forecasts made before each turning point. "The first used as a jump-off the quarter three periods before the actual reversal; the second and third started, respectively, from two quarters and one quarter before the reversal."

The essence of the test is fairly well indicated by the following selected conclusions of the report.

On the extent to which turning points were successfully predicted: "None of the forecasts made three quarters ahead manifested precise timing. In recoveries, timing was accurate only when the forecast was made one quarter before the actual upturn; prediction was accurate in two of the three cases. The results at both peaks and troughs suggest that precision is increased when the jump-off quarter is close to the turning point."

On the performance in individual cycles: "Perhaps the best performance at cyclical turning points was in the 1957-58 period. Forecasts two and three quarters before the fourth quarter 1957 decline showed a contraction in activity in the *third* quarter [that is, one quarter too soon]. The forecast made one quarter before the actual turning point predicted it correctly. . . .

"Beginning two quarters ahead, the model also predicted the 1958 upturn and to some extent its strength. Of particular interest is the forecast made two quarters before the upturn began. It shows a continuation in the decline of real G.N.P. for one more quarter, followed by a leveling off prior to recovery. The forecast one quarter before the upturn correctly predicted recovery.

"The forecasts for the 1953-54 recovery were least satisfactory, though still relatively useful. All forecasts, including the one made three ahead, showed a recession but in each case one quarter later than it actually occurred. . . . A continuation of the decline in constant dollar G.N.P. was forecast at the trough."

For an expression of the relative magnitude of the errors made in predicting the major components of G.N.P., the following tabulation may suffice. It supplies the range of low-high quarterly errors for selected items made by the model during the 1953-65 period, together with the 1965 annual values of those items.

41

Compared with the actual magnitudes of G.N.P., disposable income and consumption expenditures, these high and
low prediction errors are not large. In the case of G.N.P. the

Table 4. *Range of Quarterly Errors in Predicting G.N.P.
Components by Model 1953-1965 (in Billion
Dollars)*

	Low	High	1965
	—6.9	+ 8.1	676
Disposable Personal Income	—5.9	+ 9.2	610
Personal Consumption Expenditure	—4.9	+11.9	429
Fixed Investment			
Non-residential	—2.5	+ 1.7	70
Residential	—3.3	+ 1.7	28
Change in Business Inventories	—3.5	+ 4.5	8
Net Exports	—2.1	+ 2.1	7
Price Deflator, 1958 = 100	—1.5	+ 1.7	111

highest quarterly error of $8.1 billion represents only 1.2 per
cent, for disposable income the error was 1.5 per cent and
for consumption expenditures, 2.8 per cent. In view of the
importance of changes in business inventories, it must be
noted that the highest error, $4.5 billion, is quite large, over
50 per cent, compared with the average change in 1965. Similarly, with net exports, where the high error was about 30
per cent compared with the net figure for 1965.

Forecasting the price factors in the G.N.P. components
is also a troublesome problem. While the high error was 1.7
points, or about 1.5 per cent, in comparison with the 1965
index, in terms of the potential overstatement in the 1965
G.N.P., it would be the equivalent of $10 billion.

A more accurate test of the model, as viewed by the Department of Commerce model-builders, is its application to
1965, a year beyond the period for which the forecasting equations were developed. The model estimated G.N.P. at $677.4

billion, only $1.1 billion over the actual, but an error of 2.3 per cent in predicting the change of $47.6 billion over 1964. The change from the fourth quarter 1964 to the fourth quarter 1965 was only $0.5 billion, or about 1 per cent.

In the estimates of the major components for the fourth quarter 1965, the 1963-64 based model showed less than 1 per cent difference from actual in the case of G.N.P., but a 4 per cent error in private domestic investment, resulting chiefly from a 40 per cent understatement of the increase in inventories, and a 20 per cent overestimate of net exports of goods and services. These and other errors, some minor, some substantial, resulted in an almost perfect estimate of G.N.P. in current dollars and a $7 billion, or 1 per cent understatement of G.N.P. in constant prices. The error in the latter is traceable mostly to a 1.2 per cent overestimate of the general price level.

The Department of Commerce model-builders concluded from this that the inadequacies of the price and wage determination in their model, as well as in models of others, call for improvement in specifying the wage and price fixations, monetary equations and the equations for inventories, man hours and imports.

This, then, is how far business forecasters have come with model-building. There is no doubt about their ability to reconstruct the past experience of the economy in many of its details and to make quarterly forecasts no more than a year in advance. Leading indicators and other anticipatory economic variables are required to produce more accurate forecasts of the timing of business cycle peaks and troughs and the magnitude of recessions and recoveries.

Model-builders may be expected to improve on their ability to predict a few quarters ahead, based on the lags and sequences among economic indicators, but forecasts beyond a year will continue to be hampered by the fact that there are no leading indicators that lead the business cycle consistently by more than a year. Long-range accuracy may be expected to improve, given peace-time government policies and programs and industry efforts to iron out both seasonal and cyclical factors, particularly in production of automobiles and the construction of houses. Forecasting would then depend more on trend projection than on the changing interplay between the various segments of the economy.

Long-Range Projections of Production Required for Full Employment

CHAPTER 4

Business forecasting beyond the range of a few quarters ahead frequently involves projecting trends. In recent years, we have witnessed the proliferation of all kinds of trend projections, for the next five years, ten years, twenty-five years, and even beyond the year 2000.

Economic trends are summations of many component factors. The proper way to project such trends is to recognize the characteristics of the components, to project them separately and then sum the projected components. This procedure forces one to recognize the emergence of new features among the components which could cause the overall trend to depart from its past and present rate of growth, or change. But it is rare in economic projections that new developments can be accurately foreseen. Long-range projections are, therefore, often based on the assumption that statistical measures of past and present trends will hold good for the future.

Many long-range projections in both industrial activity and in agricultural production have turned out to be too low or too high. The most common error is to project too low, especially in industries that have shown rapid rates of growth. Prudence often leads businessmen to assume that a rapid rate of growth must presently turn into a slower one. This was the error commonly made in the 1930's, 1940's and 1950's in projections of U.S. consumption of oil, and in the 1940's, 1950's and 1960's in projections of air travel. These errors could have been avoided, had a simple principle in trend-fitting been observed.

Determining economic trends statistically is not merely a case of fitting a straight line to a series of data so that there is as much deviation, on the average, above the line as below it. In fitting a trend line it is often necessary to bear its purpose in mind. For example, if the purpose is to determine the trend effect of technology on the yield per acre of corn, which is predominantly affected by weather conditions, it is necessary to hold the weather effects constant. For general purposes, this can be done by selecting those years in which weather was either favorable or normal or below normal. For such selected years, the course of yields per acre would reflect the effect of non-weather, or technological, influences.*

In general economic projections it is often necessary to project the volume of production of an essential commodity that would be required to sustain full employment. The Employment Act of 1946 places on the federal government the responsibility of maintaining an economic climate that would promote and sustain full employment. A 4 per cent rate of unemployment has been generally accepted as representing full employment. Since World War II, when war-time employment amounted to only 2 per cent of the work force, the rate has not been below 4 per cent except during the Korean boom in 1951-53 and during the Vietnam years of 1966-69. At the end of 1966, unemployment was down to 3.7 per cent and industrial production was at its highest level in history. It receded to 3.3 per cent by February 1969, with record-level production.

---

*I have made use of this approach in an article, "Crops, Weather, and the Agricultural Revolution," in the June 1967 *American Statistician.*

Suppose you are interested in determining the volume of steel production or of industrial production as a whole, or of gross national product that will be needed several years hence under conditions of full employment. It is not necessary to set up a complex analysis of the supply and demand factors for steel, or of the relation between production and employment in the various industries that constitute industrial production and G.N.P., and to feed these detailed historical data into a computer. An elementary step in graphic correlation is all that is called for.

The Trend and Level of Steel Production Required for Full Employment

In the case of steel production required for full employment, we can draw on an important episode as an illustration. In the early postwar adjustment period (around 1946) there were two schools of thought among government economists concerning the adequacy of steel capacity for postwar full employment. Some thought steel capacity should be expanded beyond the level that was required to meet war needs. Another group argued that war-time capacity far exceeded peace-time requirements and therefore further expansion was not needed.

Drawn into this controversy, I presented a simple historical analysis that pointed to the need for additional steel capacity, if the country were to enjoy full employment in 1950. One of the charts in that analysis is reproduced here. It shows the record of steel production per capita from 1900 to 1946. Since the question related to steel production for full employment in 1950, only part of the historical record that represented years of full employment was pertinent. Those years are circled in the chart. It is immediately clear that the

47

per capita demand for steel in years of prosperity had been a rising one. By linking the prosperity-year experiences with two parallel lines, the course of the trend was automatically determined and readily projected to 1950. It indicated for 1950 a per capita steel requirement of about 1,350 pounds for full employment. The actual experience of 1950 shows nearly 1,300 pounds per capita with employment somewhat short of "full."

Chart 5. Three Estimates of Steel* Production per Capita Required for Full Employment, United States

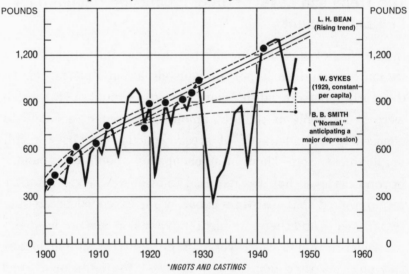

*INGOTS AND CASTINGS

The chart contains two other projections far below 1,300 pounds. They are of interest because they represent types of reasoning and method still encountered from time to time.

Mr. Sykes, then president of the National Steel Company,

48

in testimony before a congressional committee, argued against further expansion of steel capacity for we were not likely, in peace time, to need more steel than was produced during the high level of prosperity of 1929. He saw no increase in per capita demand; in fact, he thought total capacity could well be cut back (his own company was at the moment actually increasing its capacity).

Mr. Smith, then a steel industry economist, estimated still lower postwar requirements. His argument was based on the generalization that the steel industry had attained the stage of maturity beyond which the production trend should be expected to flatten out. The statistical evidence for that flattening out of the industry's growth curve he found by fitting a curve to the production record which equalized the deviations from trend. The curve is obviously held down in the 1930's and 1940's by including the depression years of the 1930's.

Trend and Level of Industrial Production and G.N.P. Required for Full Employment

A page in the monthly *Business Conditions Digest* shows almost at a glance what have been the trends in industrial production and in gross national product associated with an unemployment rate of 4 per cent and what their level should be in the near future to keep the unemployment rate from exceeding 4 per cent. The fluctuations from 1948 to 1967 in the unemployment rate and in industrial production and G.N.P. are reproduced in Chart 6.

A rate of 4 per cent, we note, prevailed at the end of 1956 and again at the end of 1965 and mid-1967. A 6 per cent rate prevailed momentarily at the beginning of 1958, at the end

49

Chart 6.   G.N.P. and Industrial Production and the Unemployment Rate, 1948-1967

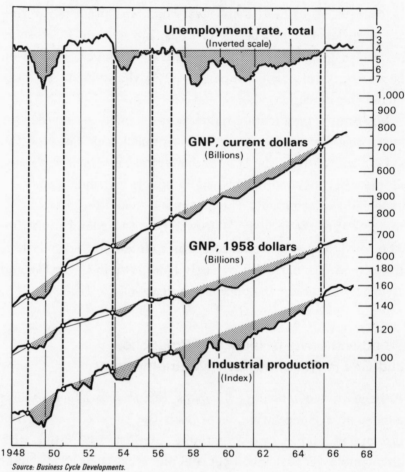

Unemployment rate, total
(Inverted scale)

2
3
4
5
6
7

1,000
900
800

GNP, current dollars
(Billions)

700

600

900
800

700

GNP, 1958 dollars
(Billions)

600
180
160
140
120

Industrial production
(Index)

100

1948   50   52   54   56   58   60   62   64   66   68

Source: Business Cycle Developments.

of 1958, during the last half of 1960 and toward the end of 1961. The technique for noting the trend of industrial production and gross national product is merely to pass trend lines through the production levels for the dates of equal unemployment rates, namely, 4 per cent. Trends parallel to the trend for 4 per cent unemployment can be determined by connecting the

50

production levels when unemployment was 5 per cent, 6 per cent or 7 per cent.

We can now interpret the relationship between industrial production and unemployment reached at the end of 1966. For unemployment to remain unchanged at the 4 per cent rate by the end of 1967, the industrial production index would have had to advance 6 to 7 per cent to nearly 170 (1957 to 1959 = 100), and if the unemployment rate were to be reduced to only 3 per cent the production index would have had to rise an additional 3 per cent, or four or five points.*

This simple device can, of course, also be used for determining the growth trend and the relation between the gross national product and the cyclical variations in the unemployment rate. The quarterly record of the gross national product of goods and services in both current and constant prices is shown in Chart 6. The trend line passes through those quarterly figures when the unemployment rate approximated 4 per cent. We are now in a position to project the trend to 1970 or 1975 on the assumption that a 4 per cent unemployment rate will prevail in those years. We may also say that these projections need to materialize if unemployment is to stay at the 4 per cent level. Incidentally, this simple method indicates practically the same increase between 1965 and 1975 as is obtained more laboriously in the previously mentioned studies of the National Planning Association, the Joint Economic Committee and the Department of Commerce.

---

*For those interested in the correlation method used here, it consists of graphically holding one variable, the unemployment rate, constant in order to determine the net relation of time to production. For a full description of the graphic method of curvilinear correlation, see my articles in the *Journal of the American Statistical Association*, December 1929 and December 1930.

This method of determining a trend by holding the unemployment rate constant immediately reveals the features of the cyclical changes around that trend; it also permits us to determine (1) how much of a cyclical rise in gross national product, exclusive of the growth trend, is required to reduce the unemployment rate by, say, one percentage point, and (2) how much of an increase is necessary from year to year to maintain a constant rate of unemployment. It is clear from both the industrial production and the gross national product relation to unemployment that the long-term growth rate of the economy is independent of the employment rate, that we can have a national production growth trend of, say, 4 per cent per year for the next five to ten years with the unemployment rate remaining constant at 5, 4 or 3 per cent. It should be observed that since World War II we attained an unemployment rate of 3 per cent only during the Korean War period.

An examination of the cyclical variations in unemployment and the comparable cyclical variations in gross national product (exclusive of trend) shows that it requires a 2.5 to 3 per cent increase in gross national product to produce a 1 per cent increase in total employment, or a one percentage point reduction in unemployment. It is also clear that, had the level of gross national product at the 1960 and 1962 peaks been at least 2 per cent higher, the unemployment rate would have approached 4 per cent instead of averaging about 5.5 per cent and government stimulus to the economy in the form of tax relief would not have been necessary.

In terms of the level of the economy at the beginning of 1967, with G.N.P. over $750 billion and unemployment down to 3.7 per cent, it would have required an additional $10 - 12 billion of production for an unemployment rate of 3 per cent and from that point on it would have been necessary to have an annual growth in G.N.P. of, say, 4 per cent (about $30 billion for the year 1967 - 68) to maintain the 3 per cent unemployment rate from year to year. The same 4 per cent rate of growth would be required for any other constant rate of unemployment.

Stock Market Forecasting

PART II:

In Part I the stock market was viewed as a national index reflecting the net changes in expectations on the part of millions as to business and profit prospects. In this section two questions are featured: Can the stock market be predicted on the basis of some leading indicator? Can it be predicted on the basis of its own characteristics? The illustrations given indicate that the answer to both questions is *yes*.

For most of the years since 1946, interest rates, a proxy for the forces of supply and demand in the money markets, have tended to lead the stock market index. Interest rates rising beyond certain levels have tended to be associated with a slowing down of market advances, and peak interest rates have generally been followed by low phases of the stock market. The movement of the stock market itself, without recourse to the outside factors that influence it, can be made to indicate how high and how low cyclical movements may carry it. To illustrate this point, two parallel trend lines marking the highs and lows experienced since 1946 are all that are required to discover that, exclusive of trend, the range between a cyclical low phase and a cyclical high phase is approximately 33 per cent.

The crucial questions concerning how to recognize as soon as possible when a bull market has ended and when the next bull will begin can also be answered by using the simplest of devices. Illustrating this point merely calls for recognizing that the first year or so of a cyclical advance establishes the bull market trend. With that rising trend established, the first *downward* deviation from it indicates that the turning point is at hand. Similarly, the downward cyclical trend can be traced. In this case the first *upward* deviation from the downtrend marks the beginning of the next cyclical advance.

For projecting the stock market a few years ahead, it is suggested that G.N.P. or net asset value per share be used as proxies for the probable trend in corporate profits and in other market factors. This is based on the simple correlation between stock prices and these two broad economic indicators that has prevailed since 1946.

Predicting
the Stock Market

CHAPTER 5

It was said some years ago that in no other area of human endeavor has so much brainpower been applied as in that of forecasting the stock market. Perhaps this still holds true today. Where else do we have so many people involved daily in trying to anticipate domestic and world-wide developments in politics, in economic activity, in weather—and trying to predict the effects of these interrelated changes and expectations on the price of securities. If expectation is a "product," then all those engaged in speculation and investment constitute the largest "industry" in the world, with its millions of investors, hundreds of thousands in banks, brokerage houses, investment institutions and clubs, and practically all corporations—all examining and analyzing facts and trends and creating expectations, determining market values. The results of all these far-flung activities are summarized hourly and daily in the standard indexes of price changes in the world's stock markets. Unfortunately the "product" is not a fixed item, with a certain shelf-life or durability. Expectations are in constant flux and respond to constantly changing conditions affecting, especially, business activity and profits.

The extent to which these expectations, measured by the stock market indexes, actually anticipate the course of business and profits has already been indicated. But note the circle we find ourselves in. It is generally understood that profits and earnings per share are fundamental to the course of individual stocks and the stock market as a whole. But we have already seen that since World War II the composite judgment of people in the stock market has fairly well anticipated the broad changes in business and profits. Predicting the stock market is therefore an exercise in predicting the predictor.

This chapter does not undertake to deal with the problem of the day to day, or week to week, or even month to month trading in stocks. In the case of business forecasting, too, our interest was not in short-run changes, either in individual industries or in business activity as a whole. So here also the interest is limited to the stock market as a whole and to the long-term fluctuations associated with the cyclical changes in business and finance, and with long-term trends.

The most common question asked when the stock market is in a rising trend is, How high will it go and when will that peak be reached? When the market is in a declining trend, the common question is, How low will it go and when will it touch bottom? Those interested in a longer view often want to know where the market will be when, for example, their children are ready for college or when they hope to retire.

These are simple questions for which all the brainpower that has been applied to the stock market and all the books and all the advisory services that you can buy ought to be able to provide ready answers. That however is not the case. Again as in business forecasting, the best minds in the stock market at any given point are in disagreement. These disagreements arise largely from their different interpretations of past and present events and different assumptions regarding future events and their probable effects on the stock market.

There is a growing tendency in this field of forecasting, as in others, to let the computer do it for you. The computer being no wiser than you, can do only what, with the data you feed it, you ask it to do. It is not just the past record that goes into this labor-saving device but also your assumptions and your mathematical instructions for handling the data. There is also a growing tendency to appraise and forecast the course of the market by making use of a variety of stock market indicators, such as the volume of trading, the number of stocks that have gone up or down, the number of shares sold "long" or "short" and other measures of the so-called technical features of the market. For the most part these are not much more illuminating than the answers one may derive from a direct examination of the stock market record itself. Is the market too high or too low? How high or low is it likely to go? Can one anticipate a cyclical downturn or a cyclical upturn? Where will the market be five or ten years hence? If these questions are of interest, the following suggestions may be helpful.

When Is the Stock Market Too High or Too Low?

This question always arises after a sustained advance and the answer is usually given in terms of price-earnings ratios. In Grandfather's day I am told the answer was simple. The right price for stocks was ten times earnings. If they were below ten, they were bargains. If over ten, they were overpriced.

There are several difficulties with this formula. In the first place it is out of date. Interest rates, the rate of growth of industries and other factors have caused investors to place a higher valuation on a dollar of earnings in recent years. It can be shown statistically (see *How to Predict the Stock Market,* pp. 43 - 49) that since 1900 there has been a long-term upward trend in the value the stock market has placed on

59

a dollar of earnings. The price paid for a dollar of earnings in the 1960's was probably three times what it was in 1900.

Another difficulty is that the price-earnings ratio depends on the relative stability of the industry involved and this is of course of extreme importance if one is considering the stocks of firms in a particular industry, such as steel, foods, electronics or utilities.

Another difficulty is with the price-earnings-ratio concept itself. It can be misleading if one is not aware of the fact that the ratio may go up because the price has gone up or because the earnings have gone down. The price-earnings ratio may go down because prices have declined or earnings have gone up. Or it may go up because prices have risen more than earnings and it may go down because prices have fallen more than earnings.

There is still another difficulty that arises when earnings are wiped out, as was generally the case in the great depression of 1932. If you divide a price, no matter how low, by practically zero earnings, you obtain a useless ratio approaching infinity. When earnings go below zero the ratio concept is of course absolutely useless.

This last difficulty of unrealistic, extremely high ratios in situations in depression years of zero or near-zero earnings can be largely met by relating price to both earnings and dividends. Dividends, generally speaking, do not disappear when earnings go to zero or into the red. For example, in 1932 the earnings for the companies in the Dow-Jones industrial index dropped to 51 cents below zero, compared with $19.94 in 1929. The price index dropped to 64 from a 1929 average of 308. But dividends in 1932 amounted to $4.62 compared with $12.75 in 1929. By combining earnings and dividends, we obtain positive ratios for both 1929 and 1932. The ratio

60

of price to earnings and dividends, it is true, rises from 9.42 in 1929 to 15.57 in 1932, but it does not disappear toward infinity.

Before examining this ratio of prices to earnings plus dividends the question may be asked, Does it make sense to combine earnings with dividends when dividends are a part of earnings? In other words, isn't this double counting in part? It is, but there may be some sense to it if you observe that many persons are interested in stocks for dividends and many others are interested in judging stocks and their prospects for appreciation chiefly on the basis of the earnings record with only a secondary concern with dividends. We do not know how many investors are primarily dividend-oriented or earnings-oriented. The combination of dividends with earnings may be thought of as an index in which earnings- and dividend-oriented investors are considered of equal importance in determining the course of the stock market.

Finally, there is the difficulty arising from the fact that prices are affected by past and anticipated earnings as well as by current earnings. Current reporting follows a long established practice of comparing price with earnings of the preceding twelve months. This tends to produce sharp aberrations in the price-earnings ratio when the stock market has reason to expect a decline in business and profits or a rise in business and profits. A number of such abrupt changes in the price-earnings ratios have occurred ever since 1940, as may be seen in Chart 7.

The thirty-year record since 1940 shows these abrupt changes in the price-earnings ratio as readily recognizable deviations from the underlying trend. The latter declined to a ratio of ten times earnings in 1942, followed by an advance to about fifteen as the course of World War II turned in favor of the

Allies. The economic uncertainties in the early postwar years brought the price-earnings ratio down to about 7.5 in 1949. This was followed by a general ten-year upward trend. By 1959 - 60 price-earnings ratios were fluctuating around 19.

Chart 7. Ratios of Stock Prices to Earnings and to Earnings and Dividends

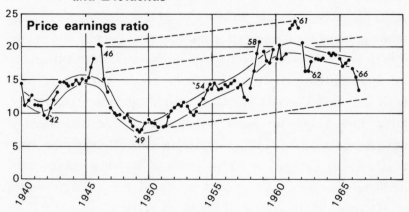

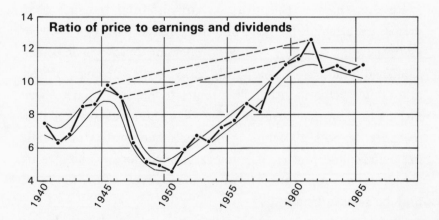

By 1966 this central tendency appeared to be at a lower level, with ratios about 17.5.

The marked departures from this central trend of price-earnings ratios occur at relatively few points in this record. It

62

is obvious that prices in the last half of 1945 and the first half of 1946 were abnormally high. During the next four years profits were revalued and devalued. During the following ten-year period of revaluation, two sharp ratio advances took place, in 1954 and 1958, years of recovery in business and profits correctly anticipated by investors and speculators. But it was not until 1961 that prices advanced sharply out of line with earnings, just as they had done in 1945 - 46. This is probably one of the main reasons for the sharp reaction in May - June 1962, at the time of the fears of adverse effects on profits, fears stimulated by the steel-price controversy between President Kennedy and spokesmen for the steel industry. The decline in the ratios of 1966 and 1956 are clearly cases of market anticipation of a decline in business and profits accompanied by government action manifesting itself in advances in interest rates.

This brief review of the behavior of the stock market in relation to earnings supplies a partial answer to the question, When are stock prices in general too high or too low? In 1945 - 46 they were too high when they rose sharply above the ratio of 15. This could also have been said of the similar rise in 1958 except that a good part of it appeared to be justified by the ten-year trend. Prices in 1961 were too high and similarly too low in 1962 as they deviated from a ratio of about 19. By the third quarter of 1966, prices were again too low in relation to a price ratio of about 17 - 19.

The thirty-year record of price-earnings ratios in Chart 7 raises the question of whether the downward central tendency since 1960 foreshadows a return to price ratios of about 10. There is no way of answering the question satisfactorily in view of the fact that the low ratios of 1942 were associated with World War II and the still lower ratios of 1949 - 50 with postwar adjustments and tax and other uncertainties. It may however be worth noting that the relatively high prices of 1946 and 1961 as well as the high phases of the central trend at about 1945 and 1960 both suggest a basic upward adjustment in price-earnings ratios. This would seem to suggest that a normal price-earnings ratio for 1968-70 could be about 17.5 (the midpoint of a range from 12.5 to 22.5).

The ratio of price to earnings and dividends from 1940 to 1967 provides essentially the same cyclical tendencies as those revealed by the ratio of price to earnings only, but with a somewhat smaller amplitude. In the annual record shown in Chart 7 the peaks of 1946 and 1961 stand out as do the low levels of 1942, 1950, 1957, 1962 and 1967. Also noticeable is the suggestion of a long-term rising trend. This too is based chiefly on the evidence of the relatively high valuations of 1946 and 1961. The downward tendency since 1960 suggests that 10 may be the normal ratio of price to earnings and dividends for 1968-70.

Earnings and dividends data, past, current and prospective, are essential in explaining and predicting stock prices of an individual company or of the market as a whole, but they are far from being sufficient. If one could predict accurately earnings and dividends five or ten years ahead, those predictions would not necessarily give satisfactory forecasts of stock prices. To satisfy yourself on that point, examine decade by decade, say from 1909 to date, the annual changes in both earnings and stock prices. In only two of the six decades will you find a reasonably close correspondence between them. The closest, believe it or not, shows up in the 1929-39 decade, the period dominated by our greatest industrial, agricultural and financial collapse. The other period is 1959-66.

By taking each decade as a whole, amazing contrasts show up. In the 1909-19 decade stock prices advanced moderately, but profits in 1916 and 1917 were three times what they were in 1909. In the following decade, 1919-29, profits rose moderately while stock prices by 1928-29 had risen about 150 per cent over those of 1919. In the 1929-39 decade both stocks and earnings tumbled and both made about the same partial recovery by 1936-37—the only period when the annual changes in each were nearly perfectly correlated. The 1939-49 period shows only a moderate advance in stock prices but profits by 1958-59 were 150 per cent higher than in 1939. The reverse of this shows up in the 1949-59 decade, a moderate advance in profits, but prices by 1959 advanced 250 per cent over those of 1949. During the 1959-66 period there was fairly close agreement between the general earnings and price advances with discrepancies in direction in 1961 and 1966.

For a brief summary of the inadequacy of earnings as a guide to stock prices for any particular year in the future, note the five- and ten-year comparisons between per share earnings and stock prices in Tables 5 and 6.

Table 5. *Per Cent Changes in Earnings and Stock Prices, by 5-year Periods, 1909-1964*

	Earnings	Stock Prices
1909-1914	−33	−10
1919-1924	−20	− 4
1929-1934	−80	−68
1939-1944	+11	+ 1
1949-1954	+20	+87
1959-1964	+35	+32

There were only two cases in six where there was general agreement between five-year changes in earnings and prices, namely 1929-34 and 1959-64.

In the six ten-year comparisons, earnings and prices changed in the same direction, increases in every case. In only one instance, 1929-39, did prices match closely the change in earnings. The others show striking differences. Between 1919 and 1929 earnings advanced 44 per cent, stock prices 154 per cent. Between 1949 and 1959 stock prices outran earnings even more. But between 1939 and 1949, the great increase in profits was only moderately reflected in higher stock prices.

Table 6.   Per Cent Changes in Earnings and Stock Prices, by 10-year Periods, 1909-1966

	Earnings	Stock Prices
1909-1919	+ 68	+ 49
1919-1929	+ 44	+154
1929-1939	− 54	− 54
1939-1949	+158	+ 26
1949-1959	+ 46	+254
1959-1966	+ 66	+ 38

These comparisons do not imply that an investment in any year will show a gain ten years later. In a growing economy, however, the chances of experiencing a gain are greater over a ten-year than over a five-year interval.

How High and How Low Will the Stock Market Go?

Most investors from time to time raise this question and a satisfactory answer would have most practical meaning. There is of course no satisfactory answer when so much depends on so many unknowns. But as is often the case, the past record itself offers useful clues. Chart 8 contains such clues. Its main feature is the Dow-Jones monthly record of prices of industrial stocks from 1946 to 1967. There is also included a monthly series representing general interest rates. Our first concern is with the stock-price record and presently with the interest record.

First note the general rise in the level of prices from the lows of 1949 to the highs of 1965-66. The cyclical characteristic dominates that upward sweep. To make this clearer, I have provided two trend lines, one that connects five of the six low points and five of the six high points.

Chart 8.   Interest Rates and the Stock Market, 1948-1967

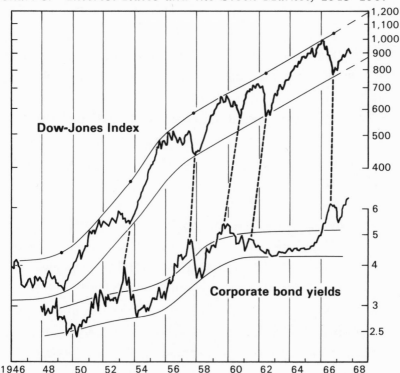

You will note that the "line of lows" goes from the lows of 1957 to those of 1962 and by-passes the low of 1960. In a presentation of the line of lows in 1962 *(How to Predict the Stock Market),* I made use of the low of 1960, but subsequent experience leads me to the presentation in this chart, which favors the practically straight line trend of the lows of 1957, 1962 and 1967.

67

The line connecting the high levels of the record I have called the 33 per cent line because it approximates the theoretical level of the market taken as 33 per cent higher than the low points of the market, and may be thought of as approximately parallel to the line of lows. These two lines neatly embrace the entire twenty-two-year behavior of the stock market.

What can we learn from this record as presented here? In the first place, note that when the Dow-Jones index reached the 1,000 level in January 1966 its theoretical low point was then 25 per cent below, or about 750. By October 1966 the projected line of highs had a value of about 1,030 and therefore the line of lows, 25 per cent less, had a value of about 770. The monthly average for October 1966 (not the lowest daily closing price) was actually 778.

What can be said about the next high point, and when it will occur? By extending this analysis into the future, it becomes obvious that the next high level of the market could approximate 1,200 if it occurred in 1970. The next low level, a year or so later, would be about 1,000. This is not to say that the next peak will occur in 1970, for the record provides no firm basis for judging when a high level may be reached. It might serve somewhat more consistently for guessing when the next low phase might occur.

If you observe the high points as having occurred in 1946, 1951, 1956, 1959, 1961 and 1966, the span between them ranges from approximately 2.5 to 5 years and, leaving out the shortest one, the range is from about 3 to 5 years. On the other hand if you take the low points of 1949, 1953, 1957, 1960, 1962 and 1966, the range is also 2 to 5 years, but if you exclude 1960 the range is about 4 to 4.5 years. If you decide to take the repetition of history as your guide (bearing in mind that even a twenty-two-year span of experience is only a very small segment of history), you might have tentatively put down 1969 - 70 for the next low point.

The actual experience in 1968 - 1969 reveals some of the qualifications to be borne in mind in making projections of this sort. The effort to check inflation with tight money and historically high interest rates prevented the Dow-Jones index in 1969 from exceeding its previous peak of 1966. It hastened the decline in anticipation of an officially planned slowdown in business activity. If interest rates should be slow in coming down, the projected range of the stock market index, based on the pre-1969 trends, would need to be lowered.

How to Predict the Beginning and End of a Bull Market

CHAPTER 6

Individuals and investment organizations have devised a number of ways for answering two crucial questions: When does a major downturn in stock prices turn into a major upturn? and When does a major advance turn into a major decline? By major, I mean the advances of 1949-52, 1953-56, 1957-62 and 1962-65.

With ample research facilities it is possible to put together the essential factors that explain the general advances and declines in the stock market, perhaps even including some measure of so-called confidence as well as of the various factors making for profits and of funds for investment and speculation purposes. With this kind of statistical correlation analysis, one would have a reasonably good idea as to which economic factors are important and need to be predicted or assumed in projecting the course of the stock market a year or more ahead. The analyses might also uncover certain economic indicators that tend to lead the stock market. Our interest here is not that kind of detailed analysis of stock price movements. It is simply to present one of the business indicators as a forerunner of the stock market and to find certain characteristics of the price record itself that could serve to anticipate changes in direction.

70

How Interest Rates Predict the Peaks and Troughs of the Stock Market

Among the many economic indicators, one, interest rates, can be of some help in judging when the market as a whole has reached its peak or its low point. Logically it should be of some help, for interest rates not only reflect the cost of money and the availability of funds for stock market purposes, but also indicate probable changes in industrial activity and profits produced by changes in central credit policies, the availability and cost of funds for industrial production, trade, construction and inventories. Interest rates reflect all these aspects of money and credit policies and in fact do seem to have value for stock market analysis and prediction. To illustrate this point, Chart 8 contains a series of interest rates based on corporate bond yields, which the U.S. Department of Commerce classifies as a coincident indicator but which I would classify as both a leading and a coincident indicator. It is one of the indicators that coincides with the stock market at the peak and leads it at the trough. Both of these facts are shown in Chart 8.

The fact that peaks in interest rates tend to lead the troughs of the stock market is indicated by the lines connecting the 1948, 1953, 1957 and 1959 interest rate peaks with the corresponding low phases of the stock market in 1949, 1953, 1957 and 1960. The lead time ranges from about six months to a year. The 1962 market decline is an exception, supporting the view that the 1962 market decline was not primarily a response to the business situation and prospects, but to the possible effect on profits if President Kennedy won out in his price-holding controversy with the steel industry and to overvaluation in 1961. The other near exception is 1966. Here the peak in interest rates preceded the low of the market by a very short time, only two to three months. The reason for this shortened lag could be that the federal government made funds available for construction to relieve the effects of the scarcity of money. In spite of this exception the interest rate series in relation to the stock market may well be worth watching as a clue to the next low point in stock market prices terminating the 1969 decline.

This interest rate series does not lead the stock market at its peak, but it has predictive value, nevertheless, provided you perform a simple operation—an operation that indicates at what level of interest rates the market begins to feel resistance that then terminates the advance.

The level of interest rates that coincides with the peak of the stock market is indicated by the interest rate level of June 1946, September 1951, April 1956, July 1959, December 1961 and January 1966. If you now pass a line through the interest rates at these points you obtain the upper trend line (the lower one is drawn parallel, passing through the low points). As interest rates reach this upper trend line, it may be said that this marks the end of the advancing phase of the stock market, and as interest rates rise above this trend they check the advance or bring on a stock market decline. In 1953, for example, interest rates rising about 3.25 per cent appear to have been unfavorable to the stock market. The stock market advance in 1956 was checked as interest rates reached 3.75 per cent. In 1965-66 interest rates exceeded 5 per cent as the advance in stock prices was checked and rose to over 6 per cent at the low point in stock prices. As interest rates fell from the peak of July 1966, stock prices reached their low point in October and started to advance with the stimulus represented by a decline in interest rates.

There is some predictive significance also to be attached to the line of low interest rates. The record permits this generalization: The advancing phase of the stock market is accompanied by interest rates first falling to the lower line and then, as the stock market and business expansion increase the demands for funds, advancing to the upper line, at which point the advance in the stock market is terminated. On the assumption that this relationship would hold good for the advance in stocks following the October 1966 low, it was possible to anticipate early in 1967 that the advance would continue until interest rates first receded to 4.5 per cent, then advanced to about 5.5 per cent. At that point the stock market could be expected to reach its next major peak.

But this pattern of expectations depended in part on whether interest rate policy would be aimed at allowing interest rates to fluctuate around the 5 per cent level, in contrast to the 3 per cent level of the early 1950's, or at allowing them to go even higher. A return to this lower level did not, in 1967, appear in prospect for the next few years at least in view of the fact that a long-term upward trend in peak interest rates (note how the 6 per cent level was attained in a series of successive peaks) would not normally be followed by an abrupt lowering of the trend in rates. It took fifteen years for the trend to rise from the 3 per cent level of 1950-51 to the 5 per cent level of 1965-66, and to the 6.5 per cent level in 1967. To the daring, this record could have suggested the even higher rates in 1968-69, and a setback to the stock market.

How the Rate of Change Predicts the Peaks and Troughs of the Stock Market

In writing about the stock market in 1962 I presented two simple devices for determining at what point in an advancing market one can foresee its end and how one might be reasonably sure that a new advance has begun. In each case I was interested in making the market record do its own forecasting. This is, of course, standard practice among chartists in Wall Street and elsewhere who believe in the Dow Theory. In fact I was interested in avoiding the various indicators of the technical aspects of the market itself, such as the number of stocks that make new highs and new lows, the number of odd lot shares purchased or sold by the "little fellows," the confidence index based on the ratio of bond yields, the number of shares in short sales, the moving averages of weeks and months and the various other aspects of the stock market.

Reviewing the long-term record, I found that a very simple measure of the rate of change in the market price index would have served excellently in anticipating all the outstanding stock market peaks since World War I; the peaks of November 1919, September 1929, May 1946 and December 1961. This does not mean that the exact month could have been foretold but that they could have been anticipated four to eight months in advance.

The device was nothing more than the change in the stock market index for a given month from what it was six months earlier. The difference can be shown either by subtraction or by a ratio of the current price to the one six months earlier. Chart 9 shows these differences during the twelve-month periods preceding the peaks of November 1919, September 1929, May 1946 and December 1961. The thin line in each case represents the six-month differences. In each case the differences mount during the first six months of the year before the peak and then become smaller during the six months just prior to the peak. The smaller differences toward the end of the twelve-month period indicate a change in the pace of the market, not a decline. These changes are here emphasized

Chart 9. Rate of Change in Stock Prices in the Twelve Months Preceding the Peaks of 1919, 1929, 1946 and 1961

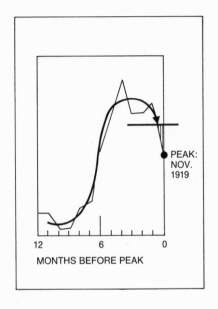

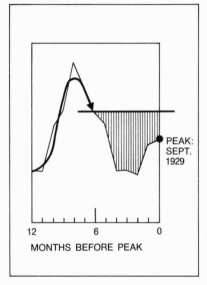

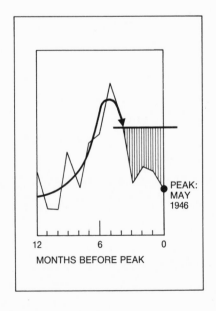

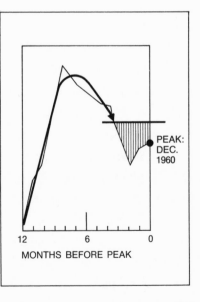

75

by the heavier trend line pointing to a horizontal line. The latter indicates when the rate-of-change line has receded by a third of the spread between the low and the high rates of change. The significance of the latter is that in these four instances waiting until the rate of increase had fallen by a third of the distance between the lowest and highest rate still allowed ample time to take advantage before the market decline set in. Another way of interpreting this chart is that one could have waited four months after the peak in the rate of change to capitalize on prices close to the subsequent peaks. For 1956 - 57 this device would have run into trouble, as any other device probably would have done, in view of the three peaks in April and August 1956 and July 1957.

I am now inclined to think that there is another way of recognizing when a general advance in the stock market has reached the period when investors could make their plans in anticipation of a possible decline. It is even simpler than taking the difference between the current price and the one six months earlier. All you need is the chart record, as in Chart 10, and a pencil.

Observe the characteristics of the five market advances since 1949, particularly the kind of trends or rates of change established during the first eighteen months after the low point in four cases and about twelve months in one. With one exception, that of 1960 - 61, you will find that if you draw the eighteen-month trend and project it in each of the four cases, sooner or later the market trend falls short noticeably, as in early 1952 and 1956, the latter part of 1959 and 1961 and the middle of 1965.

As I visualize the exercise, it shows that sooner (1961) or later (1965) there developed a noticeable failure of the market to keep pace with the initial trend, and that failure could have been interpreted as foreshadowing a decline in the market. It supplied a twelve-month warning of the January 1953 peak. It supplied a four-month warning of the peaks of April 1956, December 1959, December 1961, and an eight-month warning of the January 1966 peak. This simple, call it unsophisticated, treatment would also show similar predictive developments in practically all of the cyclical market moves prior to 1949.

The simple statistical device used in Chart 10 to observe at what point in the rising phase of a cyclical development the rate of advance slows down and turns into a decline may also be used to determine when a downtrend turns into an uptrend. In the first case we establish the slope or rate of the rising trend by graphically connecting the low points of the initial twelve- to eighteen-month advance, for it is the falling below that trend that clearly indicates a basic change in pace. In a major downtrend, a line connecting the high points marks the rate of decline, and a failure of prices to continue below it indicates a change or slowdown in the rate of decline, turning shortly into an advance.

This procedure is illustrated in Chart 11, which shows the kinds of trends that developed after five major peaks; those of 1919, 1929, 1937 and 1946. The trend line in each case begins twelve months before the peak, passes through the peak month and down to the price level twelve months after the peak. Note that the monthly price after October 1919, on its irregular downward course, remained below the trend until the summer of 1921, and by October 1921 the downward trend had definitely changed course. The downward trend of prices between September 1929 and September 1930 continued for nearly two years more. September 1932 marked the first substantial departure from that trend. In the February 1937 -

Chart 10.   Trends in Stock Prices Preceding the Five Peaks of 1953, 1956, 1959, 1961 and 1966

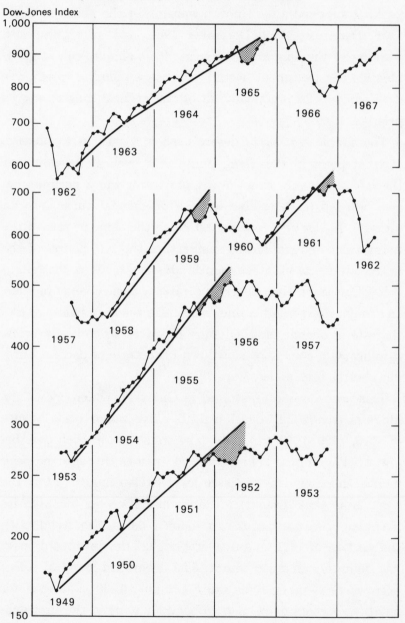

Dow-Jones Index

Chart 11.   Trends in Stock Prices Following the Peaks of 1919, 1929, 1937 and 1946

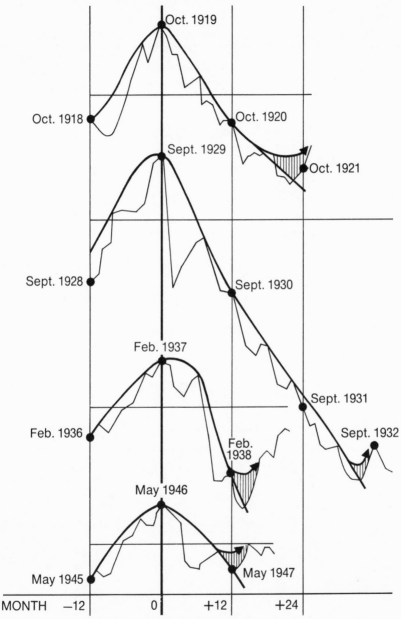

First 12 months for each period equals 100%

Chart 12. *Trends in Stock Prices Following the Peaks of 1961 and 1966*

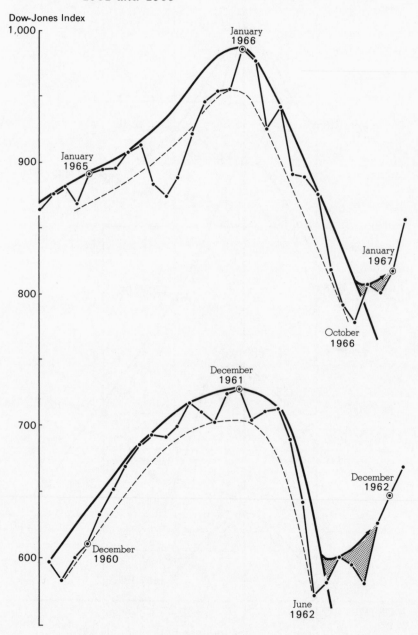

80

February 1938 decline, prices moved up sharply above the twelve-month trend after April 1938. The May 1946 - May 1947 decline was over by May 1947. The 1962 downtrend, incomplete when this chart was prepared in July 1962 turned up after June 1962, as shown in the completed record in the lower half of Chart 12.

The decline from the December 1961 peak ended in June 1962. The decline from the January 1966 peak ended in October 1966. The pace of the downtrend in the 1962 decline was broken after seven months; in 1966, after ten months. It was therefore obvious by August 1962 and again by November 1966 that the market had passed the low point in its downward course and had turned up, marking the beginning of the advances that took place in 1962 - 63 and 1966 - 67. Applied to the 1969 decline, this procedure by September seemed to indicate an impending upturn.

Projecting the Stock Market a Few Years Ahead

CHAPTER 7

What is the simplest way of projecting the general course of stock prices a few years ahead? We have already indicated what can be done statistically and graphically to define the cyclical and the long-term trend as it has developed since the war-time low level of 1942. A combination of these two components appeared to point to a 1970 level of the Dow-Jones index of about 1,200. But this is merely projecting the pre-1967 course of the stock market itself. What would be indicated if we were to project certain basic economic measures first and then estimate what market level these projections of economic fundamentals foreshadow?

What economic measures are readily available that may be projected without statistical difficulties and readily correlated with general stock prices?

Relation of Stock Prices to Assets Per Share and G.N.P.

We know that general economic conditions affect the stock market, that both volume of business and value per unit of sales determine wages and salaries, profits, aggregate sales, consumer purchases and tax revenue to government, and these as well as many other facets of the economy have their particular relation to the market. But we are not here interested in putting all these factors into a model formula to measure the relative significance of each factor, and then to project

82

each factor separately to obtain a mathematical forecast based on itemized projections. There is a more direct approach which can be illustrated by two economic series, one directly related to stock prices, one indirectly related. They are the net asset value per share and the gross national product.

The G.N.P. may be considered as the summation of all economic factors, since it measures the sum of all transactions in all purchases of goods and services by consumers, by businesses and by governments, federal, state and local. The economic factor directly related to the stock market is the net value per share, which itself is to a large extent affected by the general level of all transactions, or the G.N.P.

Chart 13 shows the course of G.N.P. in current dollars since 1942, and the trend in net assets per share and the Dow-Jones index. The course of net assets parallels the trend of G.N.P. Consequently a projection of G.N.P. provides the basis for projecting asset value per share. The course of stock prices during the period outran the trends both of asset values and G.N.P. We therefore need first the relation of G.N.P. to *asset value*, then the separate relations of stock prices to asset value and G.N.P., then the projection of G.N.P. so as to project asset value and finally an estimate of the market price, based on that projected value.

If we are interested in the year 1970, what is the G.N.P. projection for that year? The record, even though it consists of both quantity and price elements, is sufficiently stable to permit projection with some degree of confidence. The record clearly points to a G.N.P. of about 1,000 billion by 1970. Estimates by more sophisticated methods by official and private research groups also point to such a value; for example, the National Planning Association projects a G.N.P. of 1,261 billion for 1975 compared with 681 billion in 1961. The

Chart 13.   Stock Prices, Net Asset Value Per Share and G.N.P., 1942 - 1966

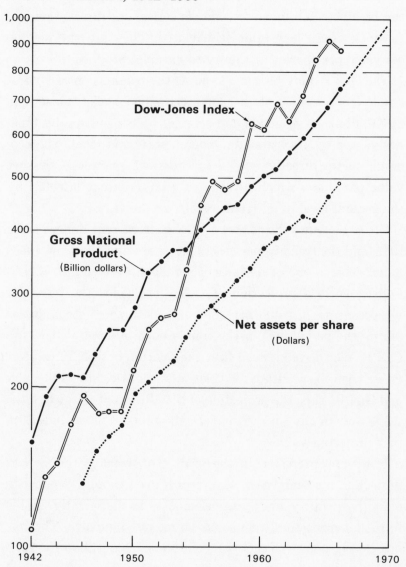

84

logarithmic trend for these two points gives 1,000 billion for 1970.

Assuming a G.N.P. of 1,000 billion for 1970, what asset value per share does it imply? The answer is in Chart 14, which shows the changing relation between G.N.P. and per share asset value. When G.N.P. was about 300 billion, asset value

Chart 14.   Relation of G.N.P. to Net Asset Value Per Share, 1946-1966

Net asset value (dollars)

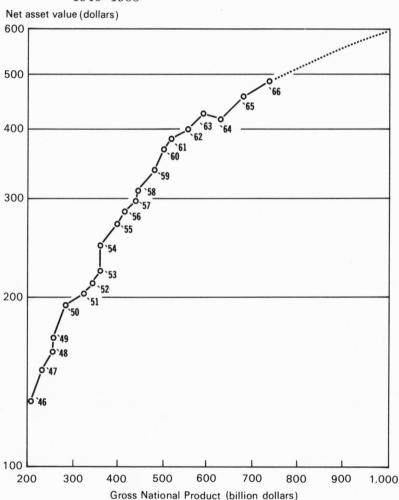

Gross National Product (billion dollars)

85

Chart 15.   *Relation of G.N.P. and Net Asset Value Per Share to Stock Prices, 1942 - 1966*

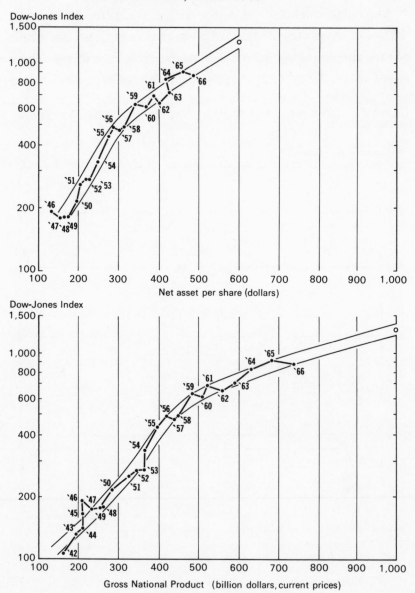

was around 200 dollars. When G.N.P. was about 500 billion, asset value was around 350, and with a G.N.P. of about 750 billion, asset value was close to 500 dollars. That the relationship between G.N.P. and asset value is in the form of a curve rather than a straight line indicates that for every 100 billion increase in G.N.P. there has been a diminishing amount of increase in asset value. Thus, as G.N.P. rose from 400 to 500 there was an increase of 85 dollars asset per share. The increase in G.N.P. from 500 to 600 was accompanied by an asset increase of about 60 dollars; the next G.N.P. increase from 600 to 700 was accompanied by an asset value increase of only 45 dollars. If this tendency continues, a G.N.P. of 1,000 would mean an asset value of about 600.

We may now examine what a G.N.P. of 1,000 billion and an asset value of 600 would mean for the Dow-Jones index. This is shown in Chart 15. We see here that the relation of both G.N.P. and asset value to stock prices changed after the mid-1950's—a slower price response after the mid-1950's than during the previous fifteen years or more. By assuming that a projection of the 1956-66 relationships may be ventured beyond the 1966 experience, the Dow-Jones index for 1,000 billion of G.N.P. may be read as about 1,300, and a net asset value of 600 also points to a Dow-Jones figure of about 1,300, according to the trends shown in Chart 15, but one should be aware of the possibility of a lower trend when the 1968-69 experience is added. That would call for a lower stock market projection.

Forecasting Political Elections

PART III:

This section on forecasting presidential and congressional elections covers a good deal of territory. Most of it, dealing with presidential elections, rests on two broad historical features that lend themselves to simple graphic presentation. For evaluating the results of presidential elections, and for predicting them, the great similarity in voting behavior between states is the essential element. This permits the use of the behavior of individual states as proxies for a number of other states and for the nation as a whole, or the use of a national indication to predict how individual states may vote. In the departures from these normal state-nation relationships, we have quantitative measures of the influence of factors such as employment conditions, religion, ethnic composition, farm and labor issues and international developments. These are here discussed in a review of my forecasts of all presidential elections from 1936 to 1968 and the short-cut methods employed.

The outstanding features in the discussion of congressional election forecasting are the simple measure of "the political tide" and the relationship between the popular vote for congressmen in mid-term years and the number of Democratic or Republican congressmen elected.

The political tide is measured by the number of congressmen from each party elected in presidential years. The departure from this trend in mid-term years, when the influence of a national campaign is not present, provides an approximate measure of the president's "coattail" influence and of additional local factors. A simple historical correlation between the change in a party's share of the popular vote and the change in the number of candidates elected between presidential and mid-term elections has been an excellent device for predicting the outcome of mid-term elections. These and other features are discussed in a review of the simple methods employed in my forecasts of congressional elections since 1938.

Predicting
Presidential Elections

CHAPTER 8

Predicting elections months or a year ahead is like predicting the business cycle or the stock market. You need an adequate foundation in the form of the historical record; you need to know why we voted as we did in the past; you need to know current developments, especially those that have transpired since the last elections; and you need to make certain assumptions as to these and other possible significant developments from the date of prediction to election day. This chapter deals with each of these essentials in relation to presidential and congressional elections.

It might be well to observe at the outset that the approach here is that of the political analyst, not that of the political journalist or columnist, political historian or political pollster. The political analyst deals with the statistical record, with quantitative effects of factors influencing that record and with estimates of the quantitative effects of the developing factors on the outcome in the light of past experience. The political journalist or columnist is essentially a reporter and interpreter of current events, while the political pollster measures current public sentiment on issues and personalities and serves the important role of bringing the historical voting record up to date for various points between the last election and the next. The pollster does not, as a rule, predict an election result. He reports on what would happen on the day the poll is taken, not next November. The journalist or columnist may predict, but only on the basis of his judgments and impressions, without quantitative substantiation. The analyses that I deal with here and have dealt with in all my political analyses begin and try to end, quantitatively, wherever possible.

Again, as in the case of business fluctuations and stock market behavior, the field of political behavior and forecasting is extremely wide, and selection of material to be presented and discussed is necessary. In the discussion of presidential elections I illustrate the fundamental relations between the voting behavior of states in comparison with that of the country as a whole. This is essential in view of the fact that it is the number of states and the electoral votes they control in the electoral college that determines the winner, not necessarily the proportion of the total votes cast nationally. In Chapter 9, "Predicting Congressional Elections," where the interest is primarily on which party gains control of the House of Representatives, the basic material is the record of the national vote for congressmen in both presidential and mid-term years.

Several actual cases are presented in which I made use of the quantitative analytical approach to presidential and congressional elections, specifically the 1960 and 1964 presidential elections and the 1954, 1962 and 1966 congressional elections. The 1960 illustration is of particular interest. It indicates why, in 1960 when the popular vote divided 50-50, when one national poll said 51 per cent for Kennedy while another equally scientific poll said 49 per cent for Kennedy, it was possible to say that the Democratic *Catholic* candidate would win.

The 1954 illustration deals with a statistical analysis of Senator McCarthy's threat to the outcome of that year's election. The 1962 illustration is also unique. In anticipating the 1962 congressional results I found it necessary to say that while in all twenty-six mid-term elections since 1854 the party in power had lost ground with but one exception, in 1934, 1962 would follow the one exception rather than the overwhelming array of historical precedent. The highly publicized experience of 1948, when my political statistical analyses pointed to a Democratic congressional victory and most likely a Democratic presidential victory as well, in sharp contrast to the showing of all polls taken during that 1948 campaign, I do not discuss here in detail for it was presented in *How to Predict Elections,* published before that election.

The most outstanding feature in analyses of presidential elections is the predominantly common response throughout the vast body of voters to overriding national issues or situations: beyond that common response there are sectional, economic, nationality, religious and other issues. It is this similarity in voting behavior which is typified in the old adage "as Maine goes so goes the nation," which I have expanded into a more meaningful description, "as your state goes so goes the nation," and now wish to expand beyond that to "as your county (or city or ward) goes so goes your state." In many instances county or ward behavior can be a direct historical replica of the national voting record. While "as Maine goes so goes the nation" was originally meant to imply that if Maine cast a majority Republican vote, so would the nation, that is not the meaning of "as your state goes so goes the nation." It refers to the fact that as the state political temperature rises or falls, so is there a parallel rise or fall in the national party percentage. There are cases where the county or state Democratic percentage never reaches 50 per cent, yet the fluctuations in that county percentage may parallel the rise and fall in the national Democratic percentage. It is the parallel movement rather than whether the two records are each above or below 50 per cent that is the significant analytical asset, both for forecasting how many states will fall into the Republican or Democratic column or by how much a particular election issue or factor caused a state or county to deviate from its normal relation to the national election.

Let us first take a capsule run-down of the past eleven elections, note the main reasons for one candidate's victory rather than the other's, then examine the voting behavior in several states in comparison with the national vote, and then, by simple correlation and other analyses, make the state-nation figures more alive with meaning in relation to the changing issues.

The Eleven Presidential Elections, 1928-1968

The first generalization that may be made on the basis of the eleven elections from 1928 to 1968 inclusive is that a candidate may get as little as 41 per cent of the two-party vote or as much as 62 per cent. Governor Alfred E. Smith, running against Herbert Hoover in 1928, received only 41 per cent of the vote, Hoover 59 per cent. In the succeeding election it was Hoover, with only 41 per cent, and Roosevelt, with 59 per cent. Roosevelt received even more support in 1936, 62.5 per cent of the vote. If we set aside these three elections and the 1964 election in which Johnson received 61 per cent of the vote, the Democratic or Republican candidates in the other seven elections received 45 to 55 per cent of the vote.

Here is the list of the eleven contests, the winning candidate underscored, and the Democratic percentage:

94

Table 7.   Two-Party Democratic Percentages in the Eleven Presidential Elections, 1928 - 1968

1928	Smith-**Hoover**	41
1932	**Roosevelt**-Hoover	59
1936	**Roosevelt**-Landon	62
1940	**Roosevelt**-Willkie	55
1944	**Roosevelt**-Dewey	54
1948	**Truman**-Dewey	55
1952	Stevenson-**Eisenhower**	45
1956	Stevenson-**Eisenhower**	42
1960	**Kennedy**-Nixon	+50
1964	**Johnson**-Goldwater	61
1968	**Nixon**-Humphrey	+50

The 55 per cent figure for Truman in this table includes the 2.5 per cent of the total vote that Democrats cast for the Dixiecrat candidate Thurmond and the Progressive candidate Henry Wallace. The 1968 percentage is Nixon's two-party vote. It was 43 per cent of the total vote in which Wallace received 14 per cent.

The main issues or factors that produced these results, these changes in the Democratic percentage of the two-party vote, include the business situation, whether prosperity or depression; legislation affecting workers, farmers, businessmen, the needy, the aged; war and peace; religion, civil rights, states' rights; and personalities.

The 1928 election—Hoover versus Smith. In the 1928 election the country was Republican and prosperous, a fact that usually favors the party in power. But in addition there was the religious issue, which caused a distortion in state-by-state voting. States where many Catholics live, chiefly in the Northeast, voted more Democratic than usual for New York Governor Al Smith. States with few Catholics and anti-Catholic prejudice, particularly Southern states, broke from the

95

traditional Democratic voting in favor of Republican Hoover.

The 1932 election—Roosevelt versus Hoover. In 1932 every state was suffering from the greatest of all depressions. The Democrats came to power with a sweeping victory, for every group in the country was experiencing the effects of the depression.

The 1936 election—Roosevelt versus Landon. In 1936 the Democratic victory was even greater, for by that time President Roosevelt had emerged as a great personality, riding the New Deal tide. Only two states, Maine and Vermont, resisted the second sweep.

The 1940 election—Roosevelt versus Willkie. In 1940 war or peace was the main issue, coupled with the concern over whether to give a president a third term, contrary to long-established tradition. Roosevelt was reelected, but his vote was reduced from the peak of 62 per cent in 1936 to 55 per cent. He had proposed packing the Supreme Court. Some unemployment was still troubling many communities. The Midwest, hoping to keep the U.S. out of the war then raging in Europe, gave increased support to the Republican candidate, while Eastern and Far Western states increased their support for Roosevelt. German-American communities also voted their pride in having "one of their own," Willkie, as a candidate.

The 1944 election—Roosevelt versus Dewey. In 1944 we were still engaged in World War II, and essentially the same issues were involved as in 1940. The fourth-term issue and some war-time dissatisfaction were offset by general prosperity.

The 1948 election—Truman versus Dewey. The 1948 election was marked by the advent of the civil rights issue and the peace issue. The adoption of the civil rights platform at the Democratic convention resulted in the organization of the States' Rights party in the South, with its own candidate. In the Northern states the fear that the Truman Administration would take a bellicose posture toward Russia produced the Progressive party, with its own candidate. These two parties drew support that would otherwise have gone to Truman, with the result that in many states the Truman ticket did not do as well as Roosevelt had done in 1944, and would have lost the election had it not been for the resurgence of the farm vote, "the green uprising." Truman offered farmers 100 per cent of parity price supports and Dewey stood for lowering them to 60 per cent.

The 1952 election—Eisenhower versus Stevenson. In 1952 the Republican party nominated the popular hero Eisenhower, charged the Democrats with "communism, corruption and Korea" as evidence of "the need for a change," with the result that in spite of prevailing prosperity the opposition, the Republicans, won the election. The states' rights issue in the South also hurt Stevenson.

The 1956 election—Eisenhower versus Stevenson. In 1956 the election was again dominated by the Eisenhower appeal and he won with a wider margin than in 1952, largely because of two international developments during the last two weeks of the campaign—the outbreak in Hungary and the Suez invasion. His gains were largely in the Eastern states. In the states west of the Mississippi disappointment in Eisenhower's promises to the farmers produced more support for Stevenson than he had received in 1952. In the Northwest the public power issue helped increase Stevenson's vote.

The 1960 election—Kennedy versus Nixon. In 1960 the election differed from that of 1956 in three respects. The popularity of Eisenhower was not a factor, since by law he could not be reelected. The Suez crisis and the Hungarian revolt were now matters of history. These two changes favored the

Democrats and tended to equalize their standing with that of the Republicans. The third feature was the religious issue. As in 1928 we witnessed the same distortion from normal patterns of voting. Protestants largely voted for Nixon, Catholics, expressing their pride in a Catholic candidate, voted for Kennedy. Nation-wide TV debates also served to equalize the rating of the two candidates, with the result that Kennedy won a mere fraction more than 50 per cent of the popular vote. The importance of the religious issue is seen again, as in 1928, in the way the Northeastern states shifted to Kennedy and the Southern states away from him.

The 1964 election—Johnson versus Goldwater. For this election the Democratic slogan was "peace, preparedness and prosperity." The Republicans argued for balancing the federal budget, cutting down on federal activities, and a more vigorous international stand against the spread of communism.

The prosperity theme favored the party in power, the Democrats. The Republicans used it in 1956 and 1960 as well as in 1928. The Democrats used it in 1940, 1944, 1948 and 1952. Reducing the federal budget has been a dominant Republican promise in all recent elections. Cutting down on federal activities in favor of the state and local governments has now become a dominant Republican platform along with states' rights and civil rights. The states' rights and civil rights issues, generally considered the most important of the issues, were, however, not new. They have colored Southern voting particularly since 1948.

The 1968 Election—Nixon versus Humphrey. In this election Vice-President Humphrey bore the brunt of the growing opposition to President Johnson's handling of the Vietnam War, at the presumed expense of domestic programs, and the mounting episodes of riots and other forms of domestic disor-

98

der which had forced Johnson to renounce his candidacy. The pre-convention prospects of a Humphrey victory were ultimately eroded, partly by the Vietnam issue especially among young followers of Senators Robert Kennedy and Eugene McCarthy, but perhaps more by third-party candidate Wallace, whose law and order platform drew away more voters from Humphrey than from Nixon.

As Your State Goes So Goes the Nation

Four states, from west to east, very well illustrate what I mean by the adage "as your state goes so goes the nation" in presidential elections. Chart 16 contains their voting history since 1928. The four states are California, Indiana, Iowa and New York. The state that comes closest to fitting this theme in the "parallel" sense is Indiana. Note how the Indiana Democratic percentage moves up and down practically paralleling the changes in the national Democratic percentages. The reason for this will probably be found in the broad similarity between the national and the Indiana economic and cultural groupings, with a larger than national proportion of the so-called conservative groups that normally tend to vote Republican. The practical significance of this fact of parallel voting behavior is that a correct sizing up of sentiment in Indiana can yield a forecast of what the national sentiment is, or vice versa. During national campaigns, polling in this state and states with similar behavior (Ohio, Pennsylvania, Michigan, Illinois) gives powerful clues to how the country as a whole responds to the two major candidates.

New York state is another excellent sample of national voting except under unusual circumstances. Such circumstances occurred in 1928, 1960 and 1964, and they are reflected in the fact that in each of these three instances New York state gave the Democratic candidate a larger share of the vote than he obtained nationally. The dates 1928 and 1960 immediately suggest the unusual circumstance, the religious issue. Alfred Smith and John F. Kennedy, both Catholics, received more than usual support from Catholics. Alfred Smith, Governor of New York state, received a relatively larger vote in relation to the national percentage than did Kennedy, but Kennedy did relatively better in his own state of Massachusetts than in New York. The unusual support for Johnson in 1964 probably reflects some lingering sympathy for the assassinated Kennedy and Goldwater's hard line regarding the conflict in Vietnam, his opposition to social security legislation and civil rights.

The Iowa example shows the impact of an economic issue that affects farmers more than voters in the industrial states. Normally Iowa, like Indiana, votes several points less Democratic than the national vote. In four of the ten elections it approximated the national Democratic percentage; in 1932, when Iowa was doubly affected by unemployment of consumers and very low farm prices because of the depression both in the U.S. and in our export markets; in 1948, when Truman promised to support farm prices at 100 per cent of parity while Dewey stood for only 60 per cent; in 1956, when Iowa voters found that the implied promises by Eisenhower in the 1952 campaign had not been carried out; and again in 1964, reflecting Goldwater's attitude toward farm price support programs and his opposition to our selling grain to Russia and its satellites.

The interesting fact in the comparison between the California and the national pattern of voting is that there is so little difference between the two in view of the great influx of population from other parts of the country, which gives California's population trend a dynamic growth far exceeding that of other parts of the country. Yet there is little evidence in the state-wide voting record that this more rapid population growth imparted a voting trend different from the national trend. The single discrepancy in these eleven elections occurred in 1956, when some Californians voted against Nixon because of his stand on the public power issue.

Chart 16. Democratic Percentage of Two-Party Vote for President, U.S., and Four States, California, Indiana, Iowa and New York, 1928-1964

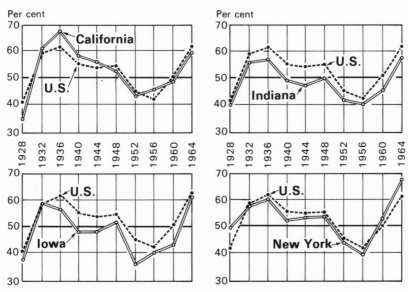

1948 includes States' rights and Progressive vote.

The Twin States

The theory that communities with the same economic and cultural composition tend to vote in the same way is beautifully illustrated in the comparisons in Chart 17. The Iowa record is almost an exact replica of the Kansas record. The

Indiana voting pattern matches the Ohio pattern very closely and so does the New Hampshire record match the Maine record, with the exception of the voting in 1964 when, I believe, the civil rights issue brought about a relatively greater Republican defection in Maine than in New Hampshire.

The 1968 election proved the continued stability of state-nation and twin-state voting patterns. This becomes evident if you extend the 1928-64 experience by adding the following 1968 two-party Democratic percentages to Chart 16:

U.S.	50
New York	53
Indiana	43
Iowa	43
California	48

and these to Chart 17:

Iowa	43
Kansas	39
Ohio	49
Indiana	43
New Hampshire	45
Maine	56
Texas	51
Florida	43
Virginia	40

Maine, for the second time in history, deviated from the pre-1960 experience by voting more Democratic than New Hampshire. In 1964 this deviation appears to have represented a greater sensitivity to civil rights issues in Maine than in New Hampshire. In 1968 the greater deviation is undoubtedly a measure of the support Senator Muskie produced for the Humphrey-Muskie ticket among his constituents.

The parallels in voting in these three sets of "twin" states are, of course, traceable to the fact that they are contiguous and have much in common in economic interest, population structure and political tradition. There are in all about twenty such sets of "twin states" outside the South. In the South, too, there are twin states; for example, Florida and Alabama

Chart 17.   Democratic Percentage of Two-Party Vote for President in "Twin" States, Maine-New Hampshire, Ohio-Indiana, Iowa-Kansas; and Three Southern States, Texas-Florida-Virginia

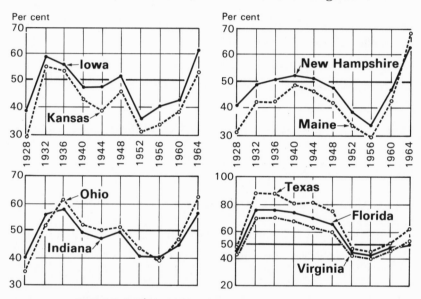

1948 includes States' rights and Progressive vote.

or Texas and Oklahoma. It may therefore come as a surprise to find in the lower right section of Chart 17 the striking parallels in voting in three states far removed from each other—Virginia, Florida and Texas. The three of them voted sharply against the Catholic candidate in 1928; show similar gradual Republican inroads between 1932 and 1948, and drastic

103

Democratic losses in 1952 and 1956, matching or exceeding the losses of 1928. The 1964 election showed gains in Democratic strength, as in 1960, but Texas, voting for a native son, showed a greater Democratic gain than that of Virginia or Florida.

The practical significance of the relatively stable voting characteristics shown in these two charts and in other similar charts (which I first presented in *Ballot Behavior* in 1940 and in *How to Predict Elections* in 1948) has been often demonstrated. In recent elections national polls in selected states have been used to represent the voting preferences in contiguous states and selected regions. In the 1968 election, when the national polls gave Nixon a very wide margin over Humphrey, I made use of polls in a dozen states which in the past had been excellent barometers of the national vote. Four weeks before the election they enabled me to contradict the national polls by saying that the two major candidates were running an even race.

Measuring the Effect of Various Election Factors

The relationship between the way the nation votes and the way individual states, counties, cities and wards vote provides the basis for measuring the effects of the various important election factors. Departures from normal patterns of voting can often be related to specific issues.

Political analysts often make their tasks complicated when simple approaches can serve just as well if not better. To unscramble the effects of a particular factor in the presence of many other conflicting factors is a real statistical art and relatively few resort to it. As a matter of fact, you do not usually need to begin with an elaborate research investigation into all details, economic, political, social, etc., for a thorough explanation of the behavior of voters in elections when you are only interested in why they "misbehave" as they do under particular circumstances. How the farmer's vote departs from the usual pattern of voting when his income is involved; how Catholic pride and Protestant prejudice distort normal behavior, how ethnic interests do likewise; how voters throughout the nation depart from traditional party preferences and oust the party in power when business depressions are allowed to develop; these are some of the voting influences that can be examined easily, as the following accounts of actual experiences indicate.

These selections deal with *(a)* the effect of the states' rights issue, *(b)* the farmer's pocket-book issue, *(c)* the dominant issues in Massachusetts (international, religious), *(d)* the religious issue, state by state and *(e)* war and the German-American vote.

HOW LARGE IS THE STATES' RIGHTS VOTE?

The issue of states' rights centers chiefly in the South and is practically inseparable from the civil rights issue. These issues affect the way the Southern states voted in the 1948, 1952, 1956 and 1964 elections, particularly the 1948 and 1964 elections. The falling off in the Democratic vote in 1948 reflects for the most part the shift of Southern Democrats to the Dixiecrat States' Rights party formed after the 1948 Democratic Convention in protest against the Hubert Humphrey civil rights platform. The Southern vote in 1964 for Republican Goldwater was another indication of the effect of the civil rights - states' rights issues. Many of the Dixiecrats of 1948 campaigned actively against Johnson.

The magnitude of the impact of this issue, state by state, is suggested in the following table of changes between 1944 and 1948 and between 1944 and 1964 in the Democratic percentages in the popular vote. The greatest defections to the Dixiecrat party occurred in Mississippi, Alabama and South Carolina. The smallest shifts took place in Texas, Virginia and Tennessee. In 1948, in Mississippi, the Democratic vote shrank by 83 per cent from that of 1944, and again in 1964. In Tennessee the Democratic vote was 11 per cent lower in 1948 than in 1944, and 6 per cent lower in 1964.

Table 8.   *The Effect of the States' Rights Issue in the South in 1948 and 1964 (Change in Democratic Per Cent of Popular Vote)*

	1944-1948	1944-1964
Mississippi	−83	−80
Alabama	−81	−82
South Carolina	−71	−54
Louisiana	−48	−38
Georgia	−20	−36
Florida	−20	−19
Arkansas	−18	−14
Texas	−14	−18
Virginia	−13	− 8
Tennessee	−11	− 6

This is the standard simple way of obtaining approximate indications of the effect of a particular issue; approximate because other issues besides states' rights contributed to the shift in Democratic voting in these two years from the more typical voting of the South in 1944.

THE FARM VOTE

Suppose you are interested in the extent to which Iowa farmers have actually shifted from one party to the other as a result of their economic interests, not as a result of their interest in all other election issues that are common to voters in all states. Their response to the general run of issues we can see in the correspondence between the record of Iowa and the national voting percentages. The effect of the special agricultural economic factor we can see, as already indicated, in Iowa's deviations from this normal relationship to the national character of the two-party gains and losses. We can see both the normal and the abnormal by arranging the presidential voting years in the order of magnitude of the U.S. Democratic percentages.

*Table 9. Democratic Two-Party Percentage of the Iowa
and the U.S. Presidential Vote, 1928 - 1968*

	U.S.	Iowa	Difference
1928	41	38	−3
1956	42	41	−1
1968	50	44	−6
1952	45	36	−7
1960	50	43	−7
1944	54	48	−6
1940	55	48	−7
1948	55	52	−3
1932	59	59	0
1964	61	62	+1
1936	62	56	−6

In six of these, Iowa's vote averaged 6 or 7 percentage points less Democratic than the national vote, which probably measures the normal relationship. In the other five cases the range of difference in the Iowa vote was from − 3 to + 1 percentage points. General familiarity with the overall features of these eleven elections gives ample clues for these five cases of greater Democratic strength than the normal difference of seven points. I have already mentioned the more favorable promises by Truman in 1948, the great impact on Iowa of the industrial-agricultural depression of 1932, the disappointment with the

107

Eisenhower Administration's performance in 1953-56 and the negative attitude toward farm problems taken by Goldwater in 1964. An additional comment is called for concerning the 1928 vote. At first I was inclined to think that the relatively greater Democratic strength in 1928 reflected Catholic sentiment for Governor Smith, but in view of the fact that Iowa gave Kennedy, in 1960, no more than normal support I have reexamined the nature of the 1928 vote not only in Iowa but in other Grain Belt states. It seems reasonably clear that Kennedy's record on farm issues prior to his candidacy for president was known by farmers as typically Eastern and consumer-directed, whereas Governor Smith's promises, following President Coolidge's vetoes of farm legislation, were taken at face value.

From this simple analysis we may conclude that an issue affecting the farmer's income, other things being equal, has a net worth of about three percentage points in a two-party vote.

THE DOMINANT ISSUES IN MASSACHUSETTS

A more complex illustration is the voting record for Massachusetts.

Here it is more difficult to find the normal relationship between the Massachusetts voting pattern and the national. The clue lies in the voting of 1932 and 1936, when Massachusetts shared with the rest of the country the woes of the 1932 depression and the benefits of the early New Deal recovery legislation. Under these circumstances Massachusetts voted 7 percentage points less Democratic than the national vote. That this may actually be the norm for Massachusetts is further suggested by the 7-point difference in 1920 and a 6-point difference in 1924.

The outstanding departures from the normal show up particularly in 1928, 1960, 1964 and 1968, obviously the result of the impact of the religious issue in 1928 and 1960; in 1964, a combination of residual sympathy for Kennedy, support for the programs he advocated and Goldwater's negative stand on domestic civil rights and international matters, and in 1968 a sort of replay of 1964.

Table 10. *Democratic Two-Party Percentage of the Massachusetts and the U.S. Presidential Vote, 1928-1968*

	U.S.	Mass.	Difference
1928	41	51	+10
1956	42	40	− 2
1968	50	65	+15
1952	45	46	+ 1
1960	50	60	+10
1944	54	53	− 1
1940	55	53	− 2
1948	55	57	+ 2
1932	59	52	− 7
1964	61	76	+15
1936	62	55	− 7

The strong 1948 Democratic vote also reflects a religious element. Truman was the beneficiary of the state Democratic position in opposition to birth-control legislation, opposition strongly supported by the large Catholic population in Massachusetts.

This leaves the abnormal Massachusetts votes of 1940 and 1944, and of 1952 and 1956, to be explained. The explanation of the first two will be found in the fact that international problems relating to impending or actual war participation gave the imcumbent president additional voter support in the East and Far West but not generally in the middle states where isolationist sentiment prevailed. This was true in 1916 as well as in 1940 and 1944. The relatively greater Democratic strength here in 1952 and 1956 will, I believe, be found in the

109

substantial support for Stevenson in the Jewish communities. This shows up also in such communities as New York, Florida and California.

From these observations we may conclude that in Massachusetts a Democratic Catholic candidate rates at least 15 percentage points more than his opponent and that international issues favor an incumbent to the extent of 5 to 6 percentage points, other things being equal.

The student with a bent toward statistics will find it instructive to make similar simple analyses for other states, especially if the tabulation is supplemented with a scatter diagram in which the U.S. percentages are plotted horizontally and the state percentages vertically.

MEASURING THE RELIGIOUS ISSUE, STATE BY STATE

The foregoing illustration shows how the effects of particular issues may be spotted and approximately measured for a given state. In some cases there are specific ways of representing an issue state by state, as, for example, the state by state proportion of Catholics in the total or church-going or voting population in studying the effect of religious pride or prejudice in 1928 and 1960; or the proportion of German-Americans in studying the effect, in 1940, of isolationism and Wilkie's German-American background.

We do not know what proportions of the actual or potential voting population fall into the various religious groups, Protestant, Catholic, Jew or Mormon. But for analyzing the 1960 election we do have data on the proportion of Catholics in the total population and this may be used as an index to observe in what states or counties Kennedy gained or lost votes because of his religion.

110

Starting with the fact that Kennedy received 50.1 per cent of the two-party vote, we can indicate the difference between what vote he normally should have received in the various states when the popular vote divides 50-50, and we may use the normal relationships between national and state Democratic percentages given in *How to Predict Elections* (p. 186, based on experience prior to 1948). For example he received 60 per cent of the vote in Massachusetts compared with 43 per cent, the normal Massachusetts figure when the national vote divides evenly for the two parties. This indicates that he received an excess of 17 per cent in a state where the Catholic population is about 52 per cent of the total. In Maryland and Ohio he received, respectively, 1 and 2 percentage points less. The Catholic proportions of the population in these two states are, respectively, 23 and 21 per cent, slightly under the national average. But in Virginia, North Carolina and Georgia, where the small proportion of Catholics (averaging about 3 per cent for the three states) is indicative of probable prejudice against a Catholic in the White House, Kennedy averaged about 20 percentage points less than normal. The Democratic defections on the Catholic issue were even greater in Florida and other states of the Deep South.

West Virginia, it is worth noting, gave Kennedy a vote of 53 per cent, only 1 point short of normal, whereas comparable Southern states went against Kennedy because of his religion to the extent of about 20 percentage points. This is fairly generally attributed to the favorable impression he made on the voters during the 1960 primary campaign.

The Ohio vote for Kennedy merits a comment in view of his great disappointment on election night when the returns came in showing that he had failed to carry that state. As reported by Theodore H. White in *The Making of the President,*

1960, Kennedy expressed his disappointment by calling attention to his hands, still red from the many handshakes in his campaigning through Ohio. He may not have been aware of the fact that Ohio gave him just about a normal vote, considering that the proportion of Catholics in the population was practically the national average.

THE ETHNIC FACTOR, THE GERMAN-AMERICAN VOTE

Just as there is pride among Catholics in a candidate of their faith for president, so was there pride among German-Americans in Willkie's candidacy in 1940 against Roosevelt. He was advertised in the German-American press as "an American whose father, mother and grandparents and whose in-laws were born in Germany—Wendell L. Willkie—a German-American whose rise is due directly to his own efforts." With German-Americans on the Republican ticket for national, state and local offices (in Illinois), "you therefore have an opportunity of voting for German-Americans, which opportunity you have so often demanded. Vote right" (*Sontagpost,* Chicago, October 13, 1940).

One of a number of tests I conducted after the 1940 election to determine the strength of the isolationist vote gathered about Willkie was in the form of an examination of the 1936-40 shift in Democratic voting in the western tier of Minnesota counties bordering North Dakota. The Democratic vote here dropped from 3 to 22 percentage points between 1936 and 1940. These losses were in direct proportion to the number of German-Americans. In the counties where only 3 per cent of the population was of German parentage the Democrats lost 3 percentage points to Willkie; where the German proportion was 15 to 20 per cent of the population, the vote shifted approximately 15 to 20 points to Willkie.

112

A similar test in Illinois gave the following results for contiguous counties in five groups, each consisting of two sub-
groups in which there was a smaller and larger average per
cent of Germans in their populations. In each case there was
a greater Willkie gain associated with the larger per cent of
Germans in the population.

Table 11.   *German Per Cent of Population and Willkie Gains,*
1936 - 1940, in Selected Groups of Illinois Counties

	Average Per Cent German	1936-1940 Willkie Gain
Group I		
a	1	4
b	4	6
	+ 3	+ 2
Group II		
a	5	7
b	12	12
	+ 7	+ 5
Group III		
a	6	5
b	16	10
	+10	+ 5
Group IV		
a	13	7
b	19	12
	+ 6	+ 5
Group V		
a	6	6
b	24	15
	+18	+11

Similar results showed up in all sections containing German-
American communities, whether North Dakota, Nebraska,
Texas, upstate New York or metropolitan New York.

The Popular Vote and the Electoral Vote

The principal use of the analyses of the way each state votes
in relation to the national vote is in forecasting the number

113

of electoral votes each candidate will obtain. If it is possible to estimate, on the basis of polls or by other means, the party percentage for a particular state and if that percentage can be translated into the equivalent national percentage, the next problem is to convert that national percentage of the popular vote into electoral votes. The relationship between these two figures has changed since 1948. Prior to that election a Democratic candidate required 52 per cent of the popular vote in order to obtain the necessary minimum of electoral votes, 266. This difference between the popular and electoral percentage resulted from the Southern states' voting solidly Democratic in the popular vote but adding no additional electoral votes in the electoral college. Since the anti civil rights and pro states' rights vote in 1948, the inroads made by Eisenhower in the Southern states and the intensified states' rights and civil rights issues have practically converted the South to two-party voting. In recent elections a number of Southern states have voted within the 45-55 per cent range, as most Northern states tend to do.

It is true that Kennedy, with 50.1 per cent of the popular vote, received 303 electoral votes. With an additional fifteen denied him by Alabama (6), Mississippi (8) and Oklahoma (1), the potential electoral total was 318, or forty-eight more than the minimum now required, 270. The thirty-three additional electoral votes actually received were for the most part the contribution of the Catholic vote in the Northeast. They more than outweighed the losses sustained in the South. The popular vote now required to win the necessary minimum of 270 electoral votes, while somewhat uncertain, may be inferred from the following table in which the election years are ordered according to the size of the Democratic percentage of the popular vote.

114

This record poses a problem in statistical estimating. The difficulty occurs at a most crucial spot in the array. I have already raised the question as to the uncertainty of what a 50 per cent popular vote would have meant in electoral votes had Kennedy not been a Catholic. Would he have received the minimum which, theoretically, ought to be obtained with a popular vote just over 50 per cent?

Table 12. *Relation of Democratic Per Cent of Two-Party Vote to Democratic Electoral Vote, 1928-1968*

	Democratic Per Cent of 2-Party Vote	Democratic Electoral Vote
1928	41	87
1956	42	73
1952	45	89
1960	50	303
1968	50	191
1948	52	303
1944	54	432
1940	55	449
1932	59	472
1964	61	486
1936	62	523

The 1960 result raises but does not settle this question. Nor is the historical record clear on this point. We are confronted with a wide gap in experience between the 45 per cent Stevenson vote in 1952, with only 89 electoral votes, and the Truman two-party vote of 52 per cent, with 303 electoral votes.

The problem is illustrated in Chart 18, which includes a line of relationship between the Democratic popular vote and the number of electoral votes. In estimating from this relationship we must recognize that the 1940, 1944 and 1960 electoral votes were somewhat higher and those for 1964, 1948 and 1952 somewhat lower than the line of relationship would

115

indicate. This means that if we want to estimate the number of electoral votes for a 50 per cent popular vote it should, theoretically, be 270, but past experience indicates that it could be more or less than this by, say, thirty votes, a noticeable margin of uncertainty at the 50 per cent point.

Chart 18. Relation Between Democratic Per Cent of Two-Party Vote and Democratic Electoral Votes, 1928-1964

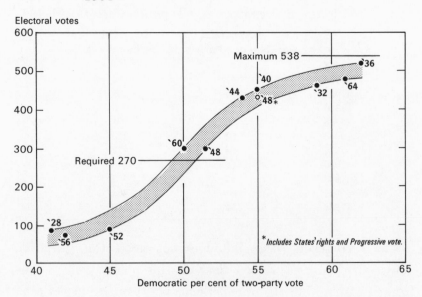

The 1968 experience in estimating electoral votes illustrates another complexity introduced by a third-party candidate. The two-party vote was practically even and each major candidate should have had approximately 270 electoral votes. Nixon received 302 and Humphrey only 191. Wallace received 45 electoral votes, mostly in the Deep South, but the popular votes he drew from potential Humphrey supporters in states outside the South deprived Humphrey of additional electoral votes. He fell short by 79 electoral votes of the 270

116

potential for the 50-50 popular vote. Thus the net effect of the Wallace vote was to throw the election to Nixon.

The difference between the popular vote and the electoral vote was nicely illustrated in an interview with Nikita Khrushchev on an NBC-TV broadcast July 11, 1967. Khrushchev said he was responsible for Kennedy's victory and had so told Kennedy in 1961. His argument was that Nixon had asked him to release our U-2 pilot, Francis Gary Powers, but Khrushchev, figuring that to do so would add 500,000 supporters to Nixon, refused to accede to Nixon's request. Since Kennedy won with a margin of only 200,000 (actually 119,000), Khrushchev told Kennedy that his refusal had given Kennedy the election. He said that Kennedy had agreed that his refusal had given him the 200,000 votes over Nixon. Actually Kennedy did not need that margin in the popular vote, for he had a margin of thirty-four electoral votes, or 11 per cent over the minimum required to win in the electoral college. For example, he could have won without the 2,800,000 votes of Massachusetts and Connecticut (thirty-two electoral votes) or without the 2,700,000 votes of Texas and West Virginia (thirty-three electoral votes).

Forecasting Presidential Elections

There is no uniform set of rules for forecasting presidential elections months before the candidates are chosen or even during the campaign period. Every election presents its own problems, its own set of circumstances and the forecasting art must be tailored especially to fit the circumstances of each election. This conclusion seems to emerge from my experiences with predicting the nine presidential elections from 1936 to 1968.

117

I have described elsewhere (in *Ballot Behavior* and *How to Predict Elections*) the steps involved in forecasting the elections of 1936, 1940, 1944 and 1948. These, therefore, need to be reviewed only briefly. More will be said concerning the subsequent five elections, particularly those of 1960 and 1968.

THE 1936 ELECTION

The forecasting device that served most usefully was the September 15 congressional election in Maine. Contrary to the prevailing judgment that "as Maine goes so goes the nation" held little meaning, I found a useful relationship between the way Maine voted for president and the way the nation voted, that the September election in Maine gave a clue to November voting in the nation. In September 1936, when polls showed a very narrow margin for Roosevelt nationally, Maine went 40 per cent Democratic. This I translated into a forecast that Roosevelt would receive 60 per cent of the popular two-party vote (he received 62 per cent) and that he would carry all states but three, Maine, Vermont and Pennsylvania. He carried all but two, Maine and Vermont.

THE 1940 ELECTION

The marked Republican gains in 1938 provoked much discussion about an incoming Republican tide, which led me to examine the nature of major political tides in the United States, the reasons for their turns and their varying rates of change. This made it possible to state at the end of 1938 that, if no major depression and no third-party problem developed in 1940, the country as a whole, in a two-party vote, would be about 54-55 per cent Democratic compared with more than 62 per cent in 1936. In the spring of 1940 the Gallup sur-

118

vey found, in two surveys two months apart, that 55 and 54 per cent of the nation wanted the Democratic party to win in 1940; and so it did, with 55 per cent of the vote.

This figure was also indicated during the campaign by two barometric county surveys conducted for me by Elmo Roper, one in Missouri, the other in California. He was interested in testing my theory that certain counties, as well as certain states, go as the nation does, a theory of barometrics which I have since put to good use a number of times.

Other considerations in 1940 had to do with isolationism and the Roosevelt third-term issue. The issue of isolationism versus internationalism, so far as it could be studied historically in the analogous election of 1916, pointed to losses in Democratic strength in the Midwest and Northwest, with offsetting gains in the East and Far West. The net effect of the third-term issue could not be adequately appraised except through current public opinion polls and these, according to Gallup, indicated that the third term presented the Democrats with no serious problem.

THE 1944 ELECTION

The 1944 election offered an opportunity to study the factor of turnout and its influence on the Democratic-Republican balance, a factor ordinarily more important in off-year congressional elections than in presidential elections. Additional Republican gains in 1942 and in special elections in 1943 were hailed as a continuation of the Republican tide that had set in after 1936 and as a foreshadowing of a Republican victory in 1944. These gains were in fact associated with unusual voter apathy in war-time congressional elections, and apathy usually hurts the party in power.

Conversely, it was clear that the Democrats in 1944 would

do better than in 1942, since turnout in a presidential election is always substantially greater than in a mid-term election and benefits the party in power, just as general economic prosperity does. As far as one could judge economic conditions, 1944 promised to be a year of prosperity. These judgments were, in early 1944, being corroborated by Gallup polls in key states. On the basis of these findings it was possible to predict, early in 1944, that the Democratic candidate would receive about 53 per cent of the popular vote. Roosevelt actually won with 53.8 per cent.

THE 1948 ELECTION

From the standpoint of forecasting, this election dominates the 1936-64 period. It presented severe tests for both pollsters and analysts. The pollsters discovered that their sampling and polling techniques were not tight enough and that voters change their minds late in the campaign. My analytical approach in *How to Predict Elections* made use of a number of elements and indications: there would be a more nearly normal turnout than in 1946; business conditions would remain prosperous; the long-time Democratic political tide had touched bottom in 1946, with 1947 local polls indicating that it had already turned up; January 1948 Gallup polls in barometric states, which I translated into a national figure, gave the Democrats 53.8 per cent in a presidential race. All these factors and indications favored the Democrats. A projection of the political tide to 1948 pointed to Democratic congressional victories in 55 per cent of the districts.

And so I wrote "all these indications prior to the Democratic troubles of early 1948 nominating conventions could be taken as pointing to victory for the Democratic candidate

120

in 1948, with a popular vote of 54 - 55 per cent in a two-party contest. Such a vote could return the Democrats to power in the lower house, giving them about 55 per cent of the seats."

There were many elements in the 1948 pre- and post-convention political developments that statistical analysis could not cope with. Two additional candidates entered the race: Henry Wallace, heading the Progressive party, and Strom Thurmond, the Southern States' Rights party. There was a deterioration in our relations with the Soviet Union and there was Truman's proposed legislation to increase military expenditures, to institute universal military training and again to draft young men into the armed service. He also proposed legislation on civil liberties which aroused the South to talk of bolting the Democratic party and, later, actually to do so. The United States reversed itself in the matter of partitioning Palestine into an Arab and a Jewish state, having secured a United Nations decision to partition. This threw in doubt the Jewish metropolitan vote and the vote of many others supporting the United Nations.

In view of these developments it is surprising that the final outcome gave 52.4 per cent to Truman in the two-party vote. In the total vote the potential Democratic share, adding in the Democrats who joined the Progressive and States' Rights parties, was 54.6 per cent, compared with the statistical indication at the beginning of 1948 of 53.8 per cent.

In an analysis of the final results of the 1948 election in *The Mid-Term Battle,* I show that Truman actually lost 185 electoral votes in fourteen states that Roosevelt carried in 1944. The States' Rights party took thirty-nine and the Progressive party seventy-five of the 185 electoral votes. Had there been no offsetting gains these 185 "lost" electoral votes would have brought Truman down to 247 electoral votes, nineteen short of the 266 required to win. But farmers in five states, Colorado, Iowa, Ohio, Wisconsin and Wyoming, gave him fifty-six electoral votes not in the Roosevelt column in 1944, more than enough to give Truman the election. If we were looking for "the one cause" we would have to say that it was the "green uprising" in favor of higher farm price supports that elected him. There was a hint of this important factor in a late 1947 Gallup poll, but statistical analysis could not have pinpointed or measured this important development.

THE 1952 AND 1956 ELECTIONS

In trying to anticipate the 1952 election results a year in advance, much depended on assumptions regarding candidates to be chosen. Predicting candidates is not within the range of political statistical analysis. But by assuming that the convention in 1952 would choose *typical* candidates, Truman, say, as a typical Democrat and Taft as a typical Republican, it was possible to visualize a Democratic victory. Business conditions promised to be good. The Democrats in 1950, in spite of our setbacks in Korea just before the election, lost only a normal number of seats, indicating that the 1946 - 48 recovery in the Democratic tide was holding. The Republican candidate who emerged in 1952 was not Taft but Eisenhower. When tested in polls prior to the Republican convention, he rated 70 per cent against Stevenson's 30 per cent. But immediately after the Democratic convention that selected Stevenson, Eisenhower lost 10 percentage points to Stevenson. Assuming this to be the beginning of a trend, it was possible to speculate that a continuation of it during the campaign might give the election to Stevenson. Polls during the campaign actually lent substance to this view. Historically it was not

122

possible to deal with Southern antipathy to an "egghead" and a civil rights advocate on the Democratic ticket. Nor is there anything in the historical record that could have given any quantitative measure of the Republican slogans, "Communism, Korea and Corruption" and "need for a change" on the ground that in a two-party country the Republicans had been out of office long enough.

These and other campaign devices, built around a popular military hero known in every home, and particularly Eisenhower's promise late in the campaign "to go to Korea" and settle the conflict, are generally credited with having been the chief reasons for Eisenhower's victory. Normally we do not turn an administration out when business prosperity prevails. It required a combination of hero worship and clever campaigning to bring about an exception to this long-standing rule.

The 1956 election was a repetition of the 1952 election, with several differences. The first is that Eisenhower's popularity was somewhat diminished. His heart attack in 1955 raised questions concerning his surviving a second term, with Nixon becoming president. Many farmers who had accepted Eisenhower's promise to get them parity in the marketplace found the promise had not meant what they expected. They were disappointed in the Secretary of Agriculture, Mr. Ezra Taft Benson, who seemed to them to be more interested in lower prices for consumers and in the consumer vote.

The statistical approach to this election followed that used in 1952. Business conditions were good in 1956 as they had been in 1952. But public opinion tests showed Eisenhower's rating again on the decline, as in 1953-54, and the health and survival issues appeared to be reflected in some shifting in voter preference and possible indecision among those who had voted for him in 1952. The effect of this indecision and possible falling away among 1952 Eisenhower voters led me to think that he might receive about 53 per cent of the vote, compared with 55 per cent in 1952. Assuming no startling surprises in campaign strategy, the Republican tide in the Congress appeared then to be not much different from that of 1954, with a fair likelihood that Democrats would retain control.

Something unusual did happen, not in strategy but in international affairs, which resulted in a greater victory for Eisenhower in 1956 than in 1952. It was the revolt against the communists in Hungary and the Israeli attack on Egypt with aid from England and France in late October. Public opinion immediately shifted toward the man in the White House. Gallup polls showed an instantaneous increase of 5 percentage points in Eisenhower's favor, unmistakably traceable to the Suez crisis in which the president sided with Egypt as did Russia. Instead of a 53 per cent vote, Eisenhower won with 58 per cent, the gain coming almost entirely east of the Mississippi. The turnout was no larger than in 1952. In practically all states west of the Mississippi, especially in the farm states, Stevenson received greater support than in 1952. The balance in Congress remained practically unchanged; instead of gaining, the Republicans lost two seats.

THE 1960 ELECTION

In March 1960 I tried to size up the election prospects for that year in a series of articles in *The New Republic*. While I recognized, in these articles, that 1960 was a year of prosperity, normally favoring the party in power, the political tide, I demonstrated, had been rising for the Democrats during the Eisen-

124

hower Administration. Nixon, the prospective Republican candidate, was behind Eisenhower's popularity rating and raised the question of Republican turnout. The farm vote prospect for the Republicans had been worsened by increasing opposition to Secretary Benson's farm programs and lower farm prices. The labor vote was also tending toward the Democratic side, especially in view of the right-to-work laws sponsored by Republican candidates in a number of states in 1958, including Ohio and California.

Since Eisenhower was by law estopped from running again in 1960, the major question, more important than the foregoing, centered on the choice of the Democrats: Stevenson or Kennedy, Stevenson a two-time loser, Kennedy a Catholic. William Jennings Bryan's experience in 1908 as a two-time loser militated against choosing Stevenson, Alfred Smith's experience in 1928 against choosing Kennedy. To the questions, Can a Roman Catholic win this year? and Can a twice-defeated candidate win? my answer, in an article in *The New Republic*, April 18, 1960, was *yes;* and I went on to give the statistical evidence.

On the religious issue I leaned on the analysis of the 1928 election in *Ballot Behavior* (1940). The central conclusion I had reached was that "other things being equal, a Catholic Democrat has a net advantage of 4 to 6 points in the eastern, middle and western states,which more than offsets losses in the South." Pointing to Gallup's findings that the country as a whole in early 1960 was 55 per cent Democratic, I added: "In rating Senator Kennedy's chances, the real question is not primarily the religious one, but whether the country as a whole will remain 55 per cent or more Democratic, what issues in addition to the religious.one would dominate the campaign and how the campaign would be managed."

125

The second question, What about the chances for a two-time loser? I answered by establishing first that the Bryan experience did not apply, for Bryan ran on an issue (monetizing silver, to raise farm prices), which proved to be too unpopular in a predominantly Republican era. I then showed, by comparing the congressional vote in 1952 and in 1956 with the presidential vote, that Eisenhower's popularity cost Stevenson 5 to 6 percentage points and that the Suez crisis cost him about 5 percentage points. Since in 1960 he would not face either of these disadvantages, he stood to fare about 10 to 11 percentage points better than in 1956. I concluded that "Stevenson's basic potential strength in 1960 was, therefore, 52-53 per cent, compared with the actual vote, in 1956, of 42 per cent." The conclusion that this meant that Stevenson could win in 1960 was supported by a poll I had conducted among 1956 Eisenhower voters in twelve typical wards in New York City, Pittsburgh, St. Louis and Los Angeles. It was found that about a fifth of them would shift to Stevenson were he to be nominated to run against Nixon. A state-wide poll of California voters, taken about the same time, produced 54 per cent for Stevenson and 53 per cent for Kennedy if either were to run against Nixon. I concluded with this: "Applying my formula 'As California Goes So Goes the Nation,' these tests suggest that [as of March 1960] either Stevenson or Kennedy could win."

After Kennedy was nominated the polls showed considerable shifting in the Kennedy-Nixon tests. At the end of the campaign Gallup gave Kennedy 51 per cent, Roper gave him 49 per cent. At that juncture, confronted by the necessity of choosing between two excellent polls (for each came within one point of Kennedy's 50.1 per cent vote), I chose the Catholic on the ground that in such a close vote Kennedy's Catholic advantage in the electoral college among the northeastern states would outweigh his disadvantages in the South; and so it did.

THE 1964 ELECTION

The statistical approach to the 1964 election early in that year was based partly on a comparison between the 1960 - 63 period and the 1932 - 35 period in which I reasoned that the Democratic tide had risen in both cases, since Roosevelt after 1932 and Kennedy after his meager victory in 1960 had both risen in public esteem. The country was more nearly at full employment in 1964 than it had been in 1960. In both cases the public generally approved the economic and social legislation that the two presidents had promoted. Furthermore, it seemed reasonable to assume that President Johnson would be the beneficiary of a sympathy vote growing out of Kennedy's assassination.

This judgment was completely corroborated by a nationwide poll in late May of 1964, partly to test whether the religious issue of 1960 was still present. The opportunity for this test presented itself in the question then being widely discussed of whether the Democratic ticket should be Johnson-Kennedy or Johnson-Humphrey. These combinations, tested against the possible Republican ticket, Goldwater-Scranton, answered both questions—which ticket would win and whether a Catholic for vice-president would make any real difference. The poll, conducted for me by the Public Opinion Surveys Corporation, gave the Johnson-Humphrey ticket a rating of 73 per cent, the Johnson-Kennedy ticket, 71 per cent. The

Johnson-Humphrey combination exceeded the Johnson-Kennedy combination by 1 to 4 points among major groups except among Catholics. Here the Johnson-Kennedy combination showed a 2-point advantage.

The survey results, based on a nation-wide sample of over 1,600 interviews, are as follows:

Table 13.   *Johnson-Humphrey   or   Johnson-Kennedy   vs.*
Goldwater-Scranton (May 1964)

	Johnson-Humphrey	Johnson-Kennedy	Difference
All Groups	73	71	+2
By Party:			
Democrats	88	86	+2
Republicans	44	42	+2
Independents	66	65	+1
By Religion:			
Protestants	69	66	+3
Catholics	85	87	−2
Jews	98	94	+4

This poll, according to the *New York Times* account of the Democratic convention in August 1964, is credited with having had some influence on Johnson's choice of Humphrey.

The 71-73 per cent rating of a Democratic ticket in May 1964 seemed unusually high. But national and state polls taken by others during the first half of 1964 showed equally high ratings. These were gradually lowered during the pre- and post-convention period as voters firmed up their judgments and responded to the candidate images and candidate positions on domestic issues and on Vietnam. Toward the end of the campaign my interpretation of various state polls by applying the formula "as a state goes so goes the nation" showed the Johnson-Humphrey ticket to be in the low 60's, carrying all but four states. The final result gave 61 per cent and all but six states to Johnson.

THE 1968 ELECTION

In reviewing the attempts at forecasting the 1968 election, it is necessary to differentiate between pre-convention and post-convention forecasts. Before the Republican convention at Miami the Democrats appeared to have the advantage. The Miami convention established Nixon's position in the polls, which thereafter changed little. The flux of the campaign following Miami shows up chiefly in shifting public response to Humphrey and Wallace. Before he was nominated, Humphrey began to regain some of the ground he had lost after the Republican convention; but then he lost the August gain as a result of the riots that adversely colored the Democratic convention. The national polls showed Humphrey dropping in popularity to a low point by mid-September as Wallace's support mounted to over 20 per cent. This was followed by a remarkable recovery in which Humphrey came within seven-tenths of 1 per cent of the Nixon vote on election day. This net Democratic gain shows up as a decline in Wallace's popularity.

Speaking to the District of Columbia Bankers Association at their 1968 Annual Convention in early June, I undertook to marshal the following statistical evidence with election prophecy in view. Before Johnson withdrew from seeking a second term, public opinion polls, national, state and local, gave him a good chance of winning, but with a considerably smaller margin than in 1964. Even after his withdrawal, opin-

129

ion polls gave Humphrey approximately a 54 per cent rating in a two-party contest with Nixon.

At that juncture the first question to be answered was, Who will be nominated? My guess was that the nominees would be Humphrey and Nixon, a guess based on the fact that in recent elections conventions appeared to choose the candidates who rated highest among *both* party politicians and party voters. Humphrey and Nixon, not Senator McCarthy and Governor Rockefeller, met this statistical requirement.

For the next question, Who will win? I called attention to the very large popular vote for Johnson in 1964 and to the comparably high popularity of Eisenhower in 1956 and Roosevelt in 1936. Following these two comparably popular elections, the winning parties lost 7-8 percentage points. This implied a reduction of 7-8 points for Humphrey below Johnson's 61 per cent. With 53-54 per cent of the two-party popular vote, Humphrey could win, depending on developments. Among the uncertainties it was necessary to recognize the possible effects of Robert Kennedy's assassination, Senator McCarthy's efforts to win the nomination, the Wallace third-party candidacy, the announcement of Rockefeller's candidacy and the course and political impact of our involvement in Vietnam.

Simplistic

The political stage was reset by the two conventions, and Humphrey's prospects deteriorated according to the Gallup and Harris national polls. Nixon still rated only 47 per cent among those who had made up their minds, Humphrey 30 per cent and Wallace 23 per cent.

In the role of political analyst trying to appraise the prophetic meaning of the September national polls, I thought that Humphrey's chances were not as black as the 15-point Nixon advantage indicated. In the first place, the national polls showed that the Wallace strength was heavily concentrated in the South. Secondly, labor organizations launched a more extensive campaign than in other elections, this time to show that Wallace was no friend of labor or of civil rights. More important than these two considerations was the evidence of polls conducted in states outside the South that in the past had been excellent barometers of the national vote.

Twelve such states (Massachusetts, Connecticut, New York, New Jersey, Pennsylvania, Maryland, Michigan, Minnesota, Ohio, Missouri, Texas and California) on a two-party basis gave Humphrey 51 per cent, in late September at the time when the Gallup poll rated him only 40 per cent. With the exception of 1964, these twelve states combined voted almost exactly as the nation as a whole in all the elections since 1936. For example, in 1936 the twelve states voted 63 per cent Democratic, the country as a whole 62 per cent. In 1956 the two figures were almost identical at 42 per cent.

This and similar evidence for individual states led me to the conclusion more than a month before the election that the race between Nixon and Humphrey in 1968 would be as close as the race between Nixon and Kennedy in 1960. In many public appearances and in a communication to the *Washington Post* several weeks before the election, I concluded on the basis of this state-nation relationship that "both candidates were equally poised in their chances for victory."

In the equally close election of 1960 it was possible to predict on the basis of the probable effect of the religious issue on the geographic distribution of the electoral vote that Kennedy, the Catholic, would win. In September-October 1968 it was not possible to do more than to point to the prospect of an unusually close race for the two major-party candidates.

131

Predicting
Congressional Elections

CHAPTER 9

Analyses aimed at predicting which party will control the Congress, the Lower House and the Senate, ought to present problems simpler than those involved in predicting presidential elections. The record is a more ample one, since elections are held every two years. But this statistical advantage is offset by the large number of individual candidates involved, 435 elected to the House of Representatives and a third of the hundred members of the Senate. Because the presidential campaign exerts its influence on congressional and senatorial races, it is necessary to separate, for analytical purposes, congressional elections in presidential election years from those of mid-term elections and to recognize that in the latter the personalities of the many candidates and the many local issues take on greater significance. In these mid-term elections congressmen cannot ride into office on the president's coattails.

In predicting the party makeup of Congress, not the outcome of individual candidates, we can rely to some extent on the behavior of large numbers and lean on central tendencies and thus avoid having to deal with so many local factors. We can examine the entire record of fifty-three congressional elections from 1854 to 1968, for the major factors responsible for the changing number of successful Republican and/or successful Democratic candidates. We can then raise these questions: To what extent do the results in general depend

132

on business conditions? What is the effect of the president's coattail? Is there a political tide that causes shifts in party control from one generation to another? How many voters stay away from the polls in mid-term years because of apathy and lack of interest in local or national issues? What effect does the falling off in voting have on the national result?

There is a minimum of statistical material needed for predicting the national results in the congressional elections. It consists of the record of the number of Democratic or Republican congressional candidates elected over a period of twenty to thirty years, the number of votes cast in total and by each major party, the per cent of the total vote cast by either party and the difference between the number of Democratic or Republican congressmen elected in presidential and in mid-term years. From this material, shown in the following charts, we can measure and mark the course of the political tide, note how turnout affects the relative strength of the two parties in the Congress, how business conditions affect the political tide, how much pulling power there is in the president's coattail, how many seats each party gains or loses for a given percentage change in the popular vote and how many districts elect congressmen with such a small margin in the popular vote that their tenure becomes uncertain.

The Political Tide

The course of the political tide is recorded in Chart 19. It shows the number of Democrats elected to the House of Representatives from 1920 to 1968. More than 217 Democrats means that Democrats control the Lower House, fewer than 218 means that Republicans are in power. The Republicans were in power, that is, in the White House, following the elections of 1920 - 28 and 1952; the Democrats were in power following the elections of 1932 - 48 and 1954 - 66. The course of the political tide is indicated by the line connecting the results of the congressional elections in presidential election years. Note that the Democrats lost control of the Lower House in 1946, with Truman, a Democrat, in the White House, and that during the Eisenhower years the Democrats controlled the Congress after the elections of 1954 - 58.

The Effect of Business Conditions

During the 1920 - 68 period the political tide shows two minor and two major waves. The two minor waves show up in the years 1920 - 28 and in 1944 - 52. The two major waves occurred in the periods 1928 - 44 and 1952 - 68.

The bottom of the Democratic tide in 1920 is associated with the postwar deflation and depression that set in in 1920. Some political analysts consider the Republican opposition to our joining the League of Nations as the dominant reason for the Democratic defeats in 1920. But there can be no argument about the cause of the major Democratic sweep after 1928. It was the great business depression, from a peak of prosperity in 1929 to a historic low in 1932. Between 1928 and 1932 the Democrats gained 147 seats as unemployment rose 22 percentage points, from 3 per cent in 1929 to 25 per cent in 1932. This suggests that nation-wide business conditions cost the party in power about seven seats for every 1 percentage point increase in unemployment.

The tide turned against the Democrats between 1936 and 1938. They lost seventy seats as unemployment rose 5 percentage points, from 14 per cent in 1937 to 19 per cent in 1938.

134

In this instance the ratio of seats lost per percentage point of unemployment is twice that of 1932, but more factors than the business reversal were involved. Voters reacted also against sit-down strikes and President Roosevelt's attempt to pack the Supreme Court in order to ensure the permanence of New Deal legislation.

In the thirty years between 1938 and 1968 the political tide was not greatly affected by changes in business conditions. They played some part in the Democratic gains in 1958 but not a dominant one.

In the long record of political shifts since the emergence of the Republican and Democratic parties in 1854, business depressions have been the primary cause of major changes in the political tide. As a rule, the party in power lost out in years of business depression. The outstanding exception was the Republican victory in 1952, when Eisenhower's popularity outweighed the condition of prosperity.

The Pulling Power of the President's Coattail

In every presidential election, and in every mid-term congressional election, the question is raised, What influence does the president have in helping to elect the candidates of his party? For a firm answer one would need a fairly complicated research project, but there is a very simple way, if an approximate answer will serve, making use of two facts. In the mid-term elections the president is not in evidence as a candidate. Therefore the difference between the number of congressmen elected in mid-term years and the number that would have been elected had a presidential election also been held at the same time would provide us with the answer.

The problem, then, is to estimate the hypothetical number

of congressmen a party would have elected in mid-term years with a president's running for office. In Chart 19 we have the trend line of Democratic party congressional strength in presidential years. This permits us to make readings for the intervening mid-term years. For example, the number of Democratic congressmen elected in 1942 fell short of the presidential year trend line by 40 and in 1944 by about 25. In 1958, with Republicans in power, the Democrats elected, and the Republicans lost, about 30 seats more than the trend line indicated. Taking into account the similar calculation for the other elections, you come to the conclusion that, on the average, the absence of presidential influence in mid-term years amounts to a difference of about 25 to 30 congressional seats. This is my tentative measure of the pulling power of the president's coattail.

Turnout in Presidential and Mid-Term Election Years

The fact that many voters who voted in a presidential election are apathetic in congressional mid-term years is recorded in the falling off in voter participation or turnout. There is less civic interest in voting for congressional candidates in mid-term election years than in voting for a presidential candidate, a lack of interest that goes hand in hand with the finding that 40 per cent or more of the voters do not even know who are their congressmen.

As shown in the 1928-66 record in Chart 20, the greatest falling off in voter interest occurred, understandably, in 1942 when this country was engaged in World War II. Many were busy with war work and many had moved from their normal voting residences.

The falling off in participation affects both parties, but the shrinkage is relatively greater for the party in power. This can be inferred from a comparison between the record of the total vote and the Democratic percentage of that total. Note that during the periods 1932-50 and 1962-66, when the Democrats were in power, the proportion of Democrats in the total mid-term voting decreased, obviously because the falling off

Chart 19.   The Political Tide, Measured by Number of Democrats Elected to House of Representatives, 1920-1968

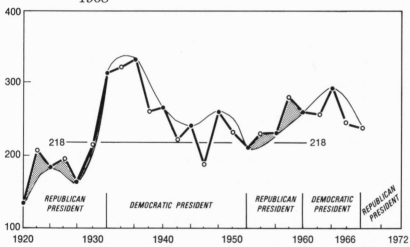

in voting was greater on the Democratic side. When the Republicans were in power in the elections of 1954-58 it was their share of the total vote that shrank. In other words, relatively more voters of the party winning a presidential election stay away from the polls in mid-term years.

As an illustration of the practical use of this fact for purposes of prediction, it was clear after the 1964 election that

137

more Democrats than Republicans would stay away in 1966, largely because the Democrats were in power and partly because about 2.5 million Republicans did not participate in 1964, thus reducing the Republican normal mid-term decline in participation. This I estimated would lower by at least 4 percentage points the 57.5 per cent Democratic share of the two-party vote in 1964. After making such an estimate, the next problem is to convert the drop in the Democratic per cent of the popular vote into the number of Democratic candidates likely to lose out. This can be determined from a simple relation between a change in the percentage of the vote and the accompanying gains or losses.

Relation of Popular Vote to Gains or Losses in Congressional Seats

At first glance the relation between the changes in the share of the popular vote a party obtains and the changes in the number of its congressional candidates who win or lose appears to be a highly variable one. It is necessary to note that the relationship is clearer in the shifts between presidential and mid-term experience than in the shifts from mid-term to presidential year experience. The former is given in Chart 20.

In this "scatter diagram" the changes in the Democratic percentages of the popular vote from presidential to mid-term election results are shown on the horizontal scale and the gains or losses in the number of Democratic seats are shown on the vertical scale. Each dot in the chart represents a mid-term election year. Thus the dot marked '58 indicates that the Democrats increased their share of the popular vote that year by 5.2 percentage points over that of 1956 and they gained 48 seats, or a ratio of 9 seats gained per percentage point gain.

Similarly in 1938 their share of the popular vote was reduced by 7.4 points and they lost 76 seats, a ratio of 10 seats lost per percentage point loss. This is the basis for the general-

Chart 20.   *Votes Cast for Candidates for the House of Repre-sentatives in Presidential and Mid-Term Years and the Democratic Per Cent of the Two-Party Vote*

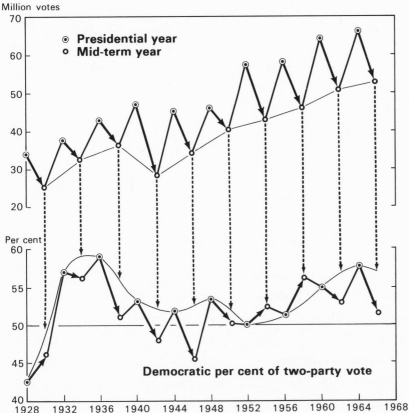

ization that, with the exceptions of 1930, 1934 and 1962, 9 or 10 seats are gained or lost for each percentage point gain or loss in the congressional mid-term popular vote.

139

Chart 21. Relation of Changes in Democratic Per Cent of Mid-Term Popular Vote from Preceding Election to Changes in Number of Democrats Elected to House of Representatives

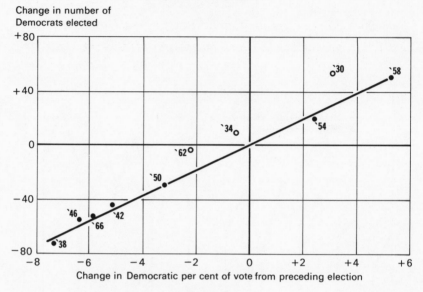

Change in number of
Democrats elected

Change in Democratic per cent of vote from preceding election

Marginal Congressional Districts

The first step in the analysis of congressional election results with a view to forecasting is to count the number of seats won by both parties by less than 5 percentage points, between 45 and 55 per cent of the district vote. In *The Mid-Term Battle* I pointed out that it is necessary to separate the marginal districts into Republican and Democratic marginals and to recognize that it is the Republican marginal seats that are endangered when the Republicans are in power, the Democratic marginal seats that are in danger when the Democrats are in power, for the political tide swings against the party in office in the mid-term election years.

140

In 1965, following the 1964 election, I introduced another modification. Not all marginal districts represent the same degree of danger in mid-term elections. It was necessary in 1965 to subdivide the Democratic marginal districts into four groups, each with distinct historical experience. Examining the historical record for these districts for the four elections 1958, 1960, 1962 and 1964, I noted that some had been won by Democrats in all four, but with declining strength. Some had been Republican districts in 1958, 1960 and 1962, and elected Democrats in 1964 contrary to previous experience. Another group consisted of districts that had elected Democrats in 1958, Republicans in 1960 and 1962, and Democrats again in 1964. A fourth group consisted of Democratic districts that had been strongly Democratic in 1958 but marginally so in the 1960, 1962 and 1964 elections. The following table shows these four groups of marginal districts in 1964, a total of fifty-five districts:

Table 14.   Democratic Marginal Congressional Districts, 1964,
Per Cent Democratic

	9 Districts	24 Districts	14 Districts	8 Districts
1958	74	44	52	59
1960	68	43	47	53
1962	62	42	44	52
1964	53	52	52	53

Of the fifty-five Democratic marginal districts, nine showed a declining trend and raised the question of whether the Democrats would be able, in 1966, to check the Republican gains. Two thirds of these were Southern districts.

Twenty-four districts, usually Republican, turned Democratic in the anti-Goldwater trend in 1964 and could be expected to elect Republicans again in 1966.

Fourteen districts elected Democratic congressmen by narrow margins both in 1958 and in 1962 and could shift back to their Republican position as in 1960 and 1962.

The fourth group of eight districts seemed to be marginally stable.

From this analysis it was possible to guess that as many as thirty-eight districts (those of the second and third groups) might elect Republican congressmen in 1966; as already indicated, the Republicans gained forty-seven seats.

While this represents a batting average of 80 per cent, it should be observed that the marginal district approach cannot be expected to pinpoint particular districts. Although in this case the Democrats lost most of the thirty-eight districts in the second and third groups, there were some that resisted the Republican trend and there were other and additional Republican gains in states where local or national issues arose after 1964 favoring the Republicans and where strong gubernatorial candidates supplied coattail help to the Republican congressional ticket.

Forecasting Congressional Elections, 1938-1966

We have seen that in presidential election forecasting there is no single set of factors that can be uniformly applied in all cases. Experience with congressional election forecasts from 1938 to 1966 leads me to the same conclusion. There are unique features in mid-term as in presidential elections and the approach used in one does not necessarily serve in another. The following brief reviews cover the progress and experience in forecasting the national results in the mid-term elections of 1938 through 1966. They indicate which of the

142

election factors noted above—the political tide, business conditions, turnout, the president's coattail influence, domestic and international issues—had to be taken into account.

THE 1938 ELECTION

The forecasting of this election was based largely on the probable effect of the sharp decline in business and employment in 1937 and a forecast that only a partial recovery would develop by November 1938. It pointed to a decline in Democratic control of the Lower House from the record of about 80 per cent in 1936 to 60-65 per cent in 1938. The Democrats dropped to a 61 per cent control. (For the relation of business activity to congressional election results see *How to Predict Elections,* Chapter 6, "When Business Cycle Meets Political Cycle.") Other issues included reaction to sit-down strikes and Roosevelt's effort to pack the Supreme Court, but their effects could not be statistically measured.

THE 1942 ELECTION

The lesson provided by this election was that political apathy hurts the party in power and this in turn had a possibly significant bearing on the presidential campaign in 1944. The Republicans claimed that their second list of great congressional gains following those of 1938 would enable them to capture the White House in 1944. These forecasts led me to examine the nature of the 1942 Republican victories in a number of districts. I found that the dominant factor was apathy, which showed itself in a greater falling off in voting among Democrats than among Republicans. The evidence was so clear that this analysis—as I discovered later—was used in setting up a bi-partisan committee, headed by the industrialist Henry Kaiser, to assure a larger turnout in 1944.

THE 1946 ELECTION

In predicting the outcome of this election the results of my analysis of political tides proved most helpful (see *How to Predict Elections,* Chapter 2, "Political Tides In and Out"). As shown in Chart 20, I had found it necessary to separate mid-term congressional election results from those of presidential election years and observed that the political tide operated at two levels. The lower level was pertinent for 1946. Its course from 1934 to 1938 to 1942, if allowed to continue into 1946, pointed clearly to a further Democratic setback, lowering the control of the House to less than 45 per cent. This actually occurred. When I called this prospect to the attention of the Speaker of the House, Mr. Sam Rayburn, pointing to the fact that he was about to lose his job as Speaker if the Democrats lost control in the House of Representatives, he dismissed my evidence, feeling sure that the Democratic Campaign Committee had things well in hand. Chart 20 is of interest for three other reasons. It indicates to me that the New Deal tide reached its peak not in 1936 but some time between 1932 and 1936. The ten-year decline from 1936 to 1946 (or the eleven-year decline from 1935) represented the duration of what I considered a typical downswing of a political tide (see p. 169, *How to Predict Elections*) and was one of the reasons for expecting a Democratic victory in 1948. The third point is that it supplies the one statistical measure we have of the effect of the president's coattail. That presidential factor is lacking in mid-term years. I have already

144

indicated that the difference in the level of results in Chart 19 represents the effect of a presidential campaign simultaneous with a congressional campaign and that the difference here is approximately 6 to 7 percentage points, representing twenty-five to thirty seats in a total of 435.

THE 1950 ELECTION

The prospects for this election are given in the analyses contained in *The Mid-Term Battle*. The measure of the effect of the president's coattail was the central reason for predicting a normal Democratic loss of twenty-five to thirty seats. They lost twenty-nine. The prospects for the Senate pointed to a Democratic loss of three or four seats. They lost six.

New features in the 1950 analyses were *(a)* an analysis of a measure of the number of voters who stayed away in the 1948 election, presumably because they did not like any of the candidates; *(b)* a demonstration that the key factor in Truman's victory was in the rural vote, whereas the gains in congressional elections centered in the industrial Northeast; *(c)* a series of state by state analyses showing the relation of the size of the vote to congressional and senatorial results; *(d)* an indication that in dealing with marginal seats as a basis for a national congressional forecast it is necessary to be concerned primarily with the marginal seats of the party in power, for the trend historically in mid-term years has been against the party in power; and *(e)* that the fortunes in gubernatorial races in general rise and fall very much like those in general congressional races.

Of interest primarily to the analyst at this stage in analytical progress is the fact that there is danger in trying to pinpoint election results in particular races without thoroughly investigating local conditions and factors. For example, the historical record for Ohio showed Senator Taft to be a possible loser but the Democrats chose a candidate to run against him without justification in experience or stature, with the result that Senator Taft won with a very wide margin.

That the 1950 Democratic losses approximated a normal figure suggests that the Korean War, in which we had met with serious reverses in the two weeks just prior to the election, had no noticeable effect. This tentative conclusion served me as the reason for assuming in 1966 that our military operations in Vietnam would not be a major factor, as apparently they were not.

THE 1954 ELECTION

The forecast of this election rested on the assumption of a normal mid-term loss for Republicans with some additional losses possibly resulting from the 1954 recession. But instead of the projected loss of about forty seats, for reasons of turnout and business recession the Republicans kept their losses to eighteen, about half the projected number. The inference to be drawn from this experience is that the Eisenhower Republican tide was still on in 1954 and had the effect of saving perhaps as many as ten to fifteen Republicans from defeat. This is not a measure of actual coattail influence but rather the possible effect of the Republican trend following their 1952 victory.

THE 1958 ELECTION

The 1958 election is of interest not so much for the analyses used in prediction but rather for the light it cast on the effect of the labor vote.

146

My forecast for that election appeared in *The New Republic* early that year. I there indicated that a Republican loss of twenty-five to thirty seats was a reasonable mid-term expectation, that a loss of forty-five seats was not impossible in view of greater unemployment and that a loss of as many as sixty seats was not improbable in view of the decline in the president's popularity and the Republican tide then in progress. In a subsequent article in *The New Republic* (September 22, 1958) I revived Maine as a forecaster, for I had found that the formula "as Maine goes in September" had

Table 15. *Per Cent of Labor Union Membership and the Vote Against Right-to-Work Laws in Three States, 1958*

	Per Cent Labor Union Membership in Potential Vote	Per Cent Voting No in R-T-W
Idaho and Kansas	9	47
Colorado and California	14	60
Ohio and Washington	22	65

worked well, especially in mid-term election years, and was likely to put in a good last performance in 1958. It led me to say that "The Maine elections now point toward the loss of sixty seats" (plus or minus the usual margin of error in this forecasting area). The Republican losses added up to forty-eight.

Just as the farm vote proved to be important ten years earlier, so I think the labor vote played an important role in 1958. In an unpublished analysis of "The Right-to-Work Issue in the 1958 Elections" I noted evidence of greater participation in Ohio, Kansas and California, three of the six states that voted on right-to-work legislation. I found that the per cent voting no on right-to-work was much higher in states with a higher labor union membership in the potential vote.

In general, Democratic senatorial candidates voting labor's position against right-to-work laws fared better in states having larger proportions of union members in the voting population. This also held true for the vote for Governor Brown in California:

Table 16. *Per Cent Voting Against Right-to-Work Law in Three California Counties and Vote for Governor and Senator, 1958*

County	Per Cent Voting No in R-T-W	Per Cent Voting for Brown (Gov.)	Engle (Sen.)
San Diego	53	52	52
Los Angeles	58	58	54
San Francisco	68	71	59

THE 1962 ELECTION

The 1962 election required a unique and interesting approach to forecasting. In January of that year President Kennedy said that history was against the Democrats because, with one exception in a hundred years, in 1934, the party in power had lost seats in mid-term elections, and this view of 1962 prospects was universally held. In considering past experience as a guide for 1962, I chose the one exception, 1934, as the appropriate analogy. Why would one set aside the evidence of twenty-five election episodes and select the one exception on which to lean? Because I saw in the first year of Kennedy's administration an increase in his popularity and a further advance in the Democratic political tide, something like Roosevelt's further gain in stature and the public support for his legislative programs. This analysis, published in January 1962, turned out to be reasonably correct. The most dramatic event that year was, of course, the Cuban crisis. In spite of that

148

unforeseen development and contrary to all expectations, the Democrats managed to hold their 1960 control of Congress.

THE 1966 ELECTION

The novelty in this election forecast is two-fold. The first is the use of a statistical correlation between the change in the per cent of the popular vote for congressmen from a presidential election to a mid-term congressional election and the number of seats gained or lost. Until late in 1966 it had been customary for pollsters to publish the results of their surveys on which party voters preferred, assuming a congressional election were held "today," but they invariably refrained from forecasting the number of seats that either party would gain or lose in view of those party preferences. The other feature is the separation of marginal seats of the party in power into several groups, indicating the relative danger of loss in each group. Both approaches seemed to point to the same conclusion: a Republican gain of thirty-six to forty seats compared with an actual gain of forty-seven. The understatement was owing to a somewhat greater shrinkage in the Democratic vote than I assumed a year or more in advance of the election.

THE 1970 ELECTION

With the 1966 election results in hand, what can be said about 1970 election prospects? The preceding analyses of presidential and congressional elections indicate that normally, as the party in power, the Republicans face a net loss of congressional seats. The mid-term winds may be expected to blow more strongly against the twenty-five marginal seats won

149

by Republicans in 1968 than against the thirty-nine marginal seats won by Democrats. Some of the 1968 Republican marginal districts have shown rising Republican trends in recent elections, which may reduce the number losing out in 1970. In addition to the normal mid-term change, there are three additional factors to be appraised: the course of business, the course of the war in Vietnam and the peace negotiations in Paris, and the progress made in dealing with domestic issues. If a business recession develops, or if drastic measures against inflation and high interest rates are resorted to to prevent a recession, it could deprive Republicans of the benefit they might otherwise gain from a substantial troop withdrawal from Vietnam and probably add confusion in the handling of domestic programs.

In view of these uncertainties we turn to a possibly useful analogy in the number of Democratic representatives elected just before and just after the previous Republican victory in 1952. The Democrats gained seventy-five seats in 1948, lost twenty-nine in 1950, lost another twenty-one seats in the Eisenhower victory in 1952. But in the 1954 election they regained nineteen. Note the recent similar sequence: The Democrats gained thirty-seven seats in 1964, lost forty-seven in 1966, and lost another five seats in the Nixon victory of 1968. As already indicated, a greater than normal Democratic gain in 1954 was offset by Eisenhower's popularity.

If one were to conclude tentatively that Republicans face the prospect of losing something less than the normal number of seats (25 - 30), that prospect would obviously need to be reappraised as international and domestic uncertainties take on more definite shape and as public opinion surveys throw light on the shifts in the Republican-Democratic balance.

150

Weather and Crop Forecasting

PART IV:

Forecasting weather and crops takes us into an uncharted area. Unlike the three preceding topics, this one provides neither commonly accepted theories nor examples of practice. Forecasting weather and crops a year or more in advance is, therefore, a novel exercise. For theory this section assumes that (1) behind weather and weather-affected yearly variations in crop yields per acre are natural cyclical forces, and (2) that this assumption leads to the expectation of repetitive patterns of fluctuations in weather and crop yield records. To find such historical repetitions as bases for forecasting, the standard statistical procedures for time series analyses are not adequate. Since historical repetitions may be of several kinds and may not necessarily follow rigid periodicities and amplitudes, the method used to find forecasting patterns is essentially one of inspection rather than standard statistical processing. The practical utility of these assumptions and the kinds of findings they lead to are illustrated here in six entirely different examples.

Weather and Crop Forecasting a Year or More Ahead

CHAPTER 10

This chapter, unlike the previous ones, deals with topics that belong strictly in the realm of natural phenomena. Business cycles, stock market fluctuations and political shifts are obviously the results of man's doings. Changes in weather and its effect on crops are nature's doings. In our need for forecasts of weather and crops from one year to the next or from month to month during the heating or growing season, the science of meteorology cannot as yet help us. We are thus forced to look for help in statistical forecasting based on available weather and crop records. Here we encounter the prevalent view that long-term weather and crop records appear largely to have the characteristics of random numbers and, therefore, provide little basis for forecasting. The chief purpose of this chapter is to suggest that this view may be erroneous, since there are many examples of non-randomness, of periodicities, of repetitions of patterns of year-to-year variations. These are the characteristics we should expect if weather changes are the end products of an orderly universe. Changes which appear to us to be random may, in fact, reflect our lack of knowledge of underlying orderliness.

Before presenting some of the examples of evidence that weather and crop changes are non-random and, therefore, predictable a year or more in advance, we need to note the current status of the science of weather and crop forecasting.

This forces us to look to statistical rather than meteorological help.

Meteorological and Statistical Weather Forecasting

The science of meteorology, as we are officially warned, has not yet reached the point where serious weather predictions beyond a few days in advance are possible. Consequently, for the numerous occasions where it would be most helpful to know what weather is likely to be a year or more ahead, we are advised to assume that next year's weather will be the same as it is today, or, as the next best guess, that it will be normal or average. This state of weather affairs is not particularly helpful to farmers or to the Secretary of Agriculture in planning next year's crop production to meet our domestic and foreign requirements, or to the industries whose job it is to keep us warm in winter. Nor is it particularly helpful to anyone to be advised to assume a norm or an average when possible departures from normal are the chief point of inquiry.

There are, of course, many commercial enterprises that offer long-range weather predictions, but their methods are not, for obvious reasons, available to the public. They, too, are undoubtedly limited in their successes by the fact that the processes of nature, which give us their end product in the form of weather changes, are not well understood.

Progress toward weather predictions a year or more in advance promises to continue to be slow. It was in the mid-1930's that the then Secretary of Agriculture, Henry A. Wallace, called in the forecasters of the Weather Bureau (then in the Department of Agriculture) and asked them to try their hands at supplying him with weather forecasts for forty-eight hours instead of twenty-four hours. This was the beginning of the

154

current official experiments with thirty-day weather projections now being issued by the Extended Forecast Division of the U. S. Weather Bureau under the direction of Dr. Jerome Namias.

The current status of extended (thirty days and longer) weather forecasting and the difficulties encountered were indicated by Dr. Jerome Namias in his 1966 report on the nature and causes of the Northeastern U.S. drought during 1962 - 65. After warning that the salient features of the 1962 - 65 climatic fluctuations should not be mistaken for causes, he summarized the meteorologist's difficulties: "At the very start it must be made clear that meteorologists and climatologists do not have satisfactory solutions to these problems; for this reason long-range predictions for time intervals beyond a month or season have not been considered possible by the scientific community.

"The reason for this undesirable state of affairs resides primarily in the fantastic complexity of atmospheric behavior. It seems that interdependence on all time and space scales is one of the characteristic features of the atmosphere. Everything seems to depend on everything else in a non-linear manner.

"To begin with our hypotheses, since the sun is the primary source of heat for driving the atmospheric motions, it is obvious that the normal wind patterns will vary with time of year. Thus, observed wind patterns for 30 March months will differ appreciably from those for 30 Aprils. In the second place, even though geographical features of the globe are fixed, there are sizable variations in characteristics of the land and water surfaces in the same season of different years. For example, temperatures of the surface waters of the ocean are now known to undergo fluctuations of several degrees F. between

155

the same month of different years. These variations in ocean temperature are broad-scale, so that water temperature anomalies of 3 to 6 degrees existing over areas as large as the United States may frequently be found in the Pacific. Furthermore, the areas of the continents occupied by ice and snow during winter also vary between winters. Finally, during the warm season the surfaces of continents vary with respect to soil moisture so that marginal areas may frequently be dry for a few years and then wet for a number of years. All these external boundary effects influence atmospheric behavior via the radiation received from the sun and emitted from the land of continent. One of the great difficulties is that the precise influence of these variable boundary conditions on the overlying atmosphere depends on the characteristics of the atmosphere itself (that is, its regional positioning of air masses, storm tracks, etc.). Thus the effect of an abnormality in oceanic temperatures, soil mixture, or snow and ice cover will be different according to the form of the general wind and weather systems.

"We have omitted mentioning variations in the sun's radiation, although it is conceivable that these external effects may also disturb the atmospheric circulation. This omission is purposeful because of the controversial nature of this subject and because of the lack of acceptance by the meteorological profession of alleged solar-weather relationships. While it appears that meteorologists are more likely, instead, to agree on the influence of earth-atmosphere boundary variations, the relative importance of these variations has not been conclusively established."

The kind of progress in weather forecasting that lies ahead was indicated by a panel of weathermen at a session of the

American Meteorological Society at the national meeting of the American Association of the Academy of Science in December 1966. As reported in the *Washington Post,* the vast amount of data on world-wide weather to be provided by satellites will be fed into high-speed computers to figure out what the weather will be. Within the next ten to fifteen years the panel expected "to be able to predict up to two weeks in advance what weather will be on a certain day."

Anyone concerned with policies and problems that turn on weather conditions a year or more in advance is today, therefore, forced to seek clues not in meteorology but in the statistical record of annual fluctuations in yearly and monthly rainfall, temperature and other data that may tend to repeat from one period to the next and therefore provide some basis for forecasting a year or more in advance.

There have been many attempts at trying to find in long-term weather records experiences that match a current situation, but the general conclusion that prevails today is that weather records appear to be very much like random numbers. Climatologists hold the view that, typically, annual or monthly rainfall and temperature data are at least 80 per cent random and therefore contain little that is useful for forecasting purposes. This view I am inclined to doubt.

It seems to me to be more in line with what we know about the orderly universe around us if we consider that the end products of an orderly universe as recorded in weather and crop data may contain evidence of that orderliness. Albert Einstein held the view that "God does not play dice with the Universe." Two corollaries follow: God, therefore, does not play dice with weather, and God does not play dice with crops. If there is reasonable suspicion that evidence of orderliness

157

may be found by going a step or two beyond the efforts of research so far, there is justification for making that additional effort.

Meteorological and Statistical Crop Forecasting

Since there are no official forecasts of weather beyond a few days or weeks, there can be no official forecasts of crops a year in advance. The U.S. Department of Agriculture is legally required only to report the farmers' judgment of the condition of the crops during their growing season and to estimate what the size of the crop appears to be at stated monthly intervals, assuming normal weather for the balance of the season. In this way, crop estimates may be likened to public opinion polls.

In the case of a public opinion poll, a small sample of the entire group whose opinion is sought is "scientifically" selected in order to represent the whole with a reasonably small margin of error. As a result of experience, particularly in the 1948 presidential election, pollsters now go out of their way to indicate that their results, obtained in August, for example, apply only to the day or days when the poll was conducted and are not to be taken as a forecast of the actual results on election day in November. The pollster usually precedes his question with "If the election were held today . . . " The results are usually qualified by the observation that much can happen between the time of the poll and election day.

Crop forecasting started in 1866 and should be considered our earliest form of opinion polling. By law the Crop Reporting Service of the U.S. Department of Agriculture is charged merely with the task of soliciting opinions, particularly of farmers, concerning the condition of the crop at the time

158

the survey is conducted. Typically, the U.S. Department of Agriculture obtains these opinions around the first day of the month during the growing season and interprets the farmer's judgment concerning the condition of the crop in terms of the size of the crop to be, on the assumption of normal weather, for the balance of the growing season. On the occasions at congressional hearings when the Department of Agriculture was criticized for and questioned on its changes in forecast from month to month, it sought refuge behind the law that requires it to estimate production as of a given date, and replied that later changes in estimates are therefore the result of weather changes and not the whims of the Crop Reporting Service.

Just as the Department of Agriculture cannot predict the final outcome of a crop once it has been planted, so it would be handicapped even more were it to attempt to predict crop production a year or more in advance. When it does make such projections, normal weather is always assumed with some allowance for any recent trend in yields per acre.

We have already seen that the Weather Bureau can be of little help to within-the-season or beyond-the-season crop forecasting. Except for the short-range forecasts available a few days in advance, official weather forecasting of within-season changes or changes for the following season is limited of necessity to the assumption that current conditions will remain unchanged, or that next year they will be normal.

Crop forecasts for a year or more in advance are of growing importance as the U.S. and other countries are becoming more and more involved in international commitments to aid countries affected by floods, droughts, famines and malnutrition. In spite of this need of foreknowledge on the part of both exporting and importing countries, progress in long-range crop yield forecasting is at a standstill and will undoubtedly remain so until meteorological science discovers how to bridge the seasons, how to foresee what weather will be a year ahead.

This point has been made often enough, but I am tempted to belabor it with one further comment. It is now more than forty years since the U.S. Department of Agriculture instituted the Annual Agricultural Outlook Conference, attended by agricultural economists and extension agents from every state. The central purpose of the outlook conference is to provide farmers with information to guide them in their planting and marketing plans for the following year, especially in regard to domestic and foreign demand and price trends. Basic to all this is the effect of weather on the next year's yield per acre, here and abroad. When the outlook conference was first held in 1923 it was necessary, in judging next year's supplies, to assume normal weather and normal yields. These assumptions are still being made.

Are Weather and Crop Records Random Numbers?

The researcher with "randomness" in the back of his mind, on examining a weather or crop record, may think he finds evidence of randomness and little else. The researcher with "orderliness" and "historical repetitions" in the back of his mind may think he sees orderliness and repetition where others see little.

There have been many occasions over a fairly long period when government policy questions relating to agriculture turned my interest to the predictability of next year's weather and crops. A number of these experiments, observations and actual tested forecasts are the basis for this chapter, but before presenting some of them it may be helpful to examine the characteristics of time series that are known to be the results of components of regular, repetitive, cyclical fluctuations of the kind I assume weather and crop data to be. What are some of these characteristics, and can one find such or similar features in the weather records, the basic components of which we do not know and which our statistical devices may not be able to uncover? The features that concern us here are those that are, or appear to be, repetitions in time series composed of regular cycles of different amplitudes and periodicities.

It is common statistical knowledge that when several cyclical factors, each of fixed periodicity and amplitude, are combined, the result may be an irregular-appearing series with no obvious regular periodicity or amplitude. Yet this resulting series may contain repetitive fluctuations according to the law of the combination of numbers or cycles; if you combine, for example, a three-year with a five-year cycle the same resulting sums or values will show up at intervals of fifteen years. The new series of numbers will not necessarily look like the originals but it will contain repetitions of its own and not necessarily those of its components. Furthermore, it may contain two types of repetitions: *lag repetitions,* where repetitions take place after a given time interval, and *symmetry-point repetitions,* where repetitions occur around a point of symmetry (if you join your two thumbs and fold your hands, the juncture of thumbs is a point of symmetry; the index finger of the left hand will match the index finger of the right hand, and the other three fingers of the left hand will match their opposites of the right hand). Where these features of the summed series are recognized, they may be used for forecasting beyond the last point of the series.

161

A simple example in Chart 22 will illustrate the point that *random-appearing* series related to natural phenomena such as variations in rainfall or temperature and in crop yields resulting from weather variations may contain non-random repetitive variations. In short, we have a series of numbers, which, for the purposes of this illustration, we may consider as yearly rainfall, temperature or crop yield variations. The years run from 1 to 49.

Chart 22.   Random-Appearing Numbers Produced by Summation of Four Regular Cyclical Patterns of Different Lengths and Amplitudes

Four cycles
a. 0–5–0
b. 1–3–6–1
c. 0–2–4–2–0
d. 1–2–4–6–8–6–4–2–1

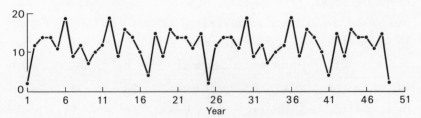

Scanning this series as one would normally do, we look for trends and cyclical tendencies. The trend is horizontal. Cyclical variations, if they exist, are not clear, and there appear to be no recurrences at fixed intervals. The first two lowest points are separated by sixteen years and the third by eight years. The first two high points are separated by six years, the second and third by eighteen years and the third and fourth by six years. There are only nine extreme observations that fall outside the central range of variations from 7 to 16, about

162

the proportion that one might expect in a set of forty-nine random numbers.

On further examination, noting how relatively low are Years 9, 17 and 32, as well as the more extreme lows, there is a suggestion of a possible eight-year cycle. A moving average would show an approximate eight-year cyclical tendency.

As for patterns of yearly variations that appear to be repetitions of earlier segments of the record, there also seems to be little evidence. But, examining more closely, we note that the variations for the eight years following Year 9 are a fair replica of the variations for the years prior to Year 9, extending back to Year 1. The high degree of correspondence or correlation, using Year 9 as a point of departure, is seen in the following two rows:

Table 17. Example of Repetition in a Constructed but Random-Appearing Series of Numbers

(a)	**Years 9-17**	7 — 10 — 11 — 19 — 9 — 16 — 14 — 10 — 4
(b)	**Years 9-1**	7 — 12 — 9 — 19 — 11 — 14 — 14 — 12 — 2
	Difference (a—b)	−2 +2 0 −2 +2 0 −2 +2

There is still another pattern that is a repetition of an earlier one. Note the points for Years 25 to 33 and compare them with 1 to 9. The comparison in this case, with a lag of twenty-four years, is between identical numbers—a case of perfect correlation.

At this point the question arises, Can the sequence of years after Year 9 be used to predict the series one or more years following Year 33, on the assumption that there may be something in the series that repeats for more than the so far observed eight years? The answer is yes—in fact, we now see that the entire segment of the record from 25 to 49 is an exact replica of the first segment 1 to 25.

This series of forty-nine numbers, which contains evidence of an eight-year cycle, two cases of highly correlated point-repetitions and a sequence of twenty-four items that are an exact repetition of the twenty-four preceding items is, of course, a hypothetical series. It is the sum of four regular cycles extended to represent forty-nine years. One cycle has a periodicity of two years, the other three have periodicities of three, four and eight years. Their amplitudes are, respectively, 0 to 5, 0 to 6, 1 to 4 and 1 to 8. Their sums for the first nine years are obtained thus:

Table 18.   *Example of First Nine Sums in a Series of Four Regular Cycles*

(a)	0 —	5 —	0 —	5 —	0 —	5 —	0 —	5 —	0
(b)	1 —	3 —	6 —	1 —	3 —	6 —	1 —	3 —	6
(c)	0 —	2 —	4 —	2 —	0 —	2 —	4 —	2 —	0
(d)	1 —	2 —	4 —	6 —	8 —	6 —	4 —	2 —	1
Sum	2 —	12 —	14 —	14 —	11 —	19 —	9 —	12 —	7

We can now see why the series of sums contains evidence of an eight-year cycle, why the other periodicities do not appear and why exact repetition occurs after an interval of twenty-four years. The eight-year-cycle component is more pronounced, has a wider amplitude than the other three, and the latter are lost sight of because they tend to offset each other. The twenty-four-year repetition results from the fact that cycles of three and eight years converge in twenty-four years according to the law of combinations. The main point of this exercise is to show that even if we do not know what the cyclical components of a time series are, there may in fact be certain repetitive sequences useful for purposes of prediction.

In actual practice, researchers in time series problems, observing only one or two repetitions of patterns of fluctuations, will invariably discard them on the ground that more cases of repetitions are needed to warrant prediction. But how many repetitions are statistically necessary to establish the fact that they are real? And may not only one or two repetitions have practical value in projecting the next point or two of a currently emerging repetitive pattern? The obvious answer is no, but this judgment may be too hasty. Consider, for example, the analysis of a weather record or crop yield record containing eighty annual observations. How many exact repetitions should be found before they can be used in forecasting? If the series contains cyclical components with periodicities of five and seven, exact repetitions will show up after a lag or interval of thirty-five years; in a record that spans eighty years there can be only two complete patterns of fluctuation where the second is an exact repetition of the first. The variations in the last few years of an eighty-year series composed of five- and seven-year cycles would be exact repetitions of only two other periods, the first part of the first thirty-five-year period and the first part of the second thirty-five-year period.

Our hypothetical example of the combination of cycles producing a non-cyclical series probably oversimplifies the processes in nature. There are undoubtedly many cycles of years and fractions of years and short and long trends which combine to baffle the search for regular, non-random characteristics.

In the examples in Chapter 11, derived from actual weather and crop series, we will observe a variety of cases of repetitions, instances where patterns of fluctuations have repeated earlier patterns once or more than once, where repeating patterns have prevailed for ten to twenty years, long enough to indicate a high degree of orderliness, and so of usefulness.

Examples of Weather and Crop Forecasts a Year or More in Advance

CHAPTER 11

The examples of the predictability of weather and crops a year or more ahead have been drawn from a wide field of natural phenomena. The records used are annual, monthly and daily. They pertain to regions, states, districts and cities and represent variations in rainfall, temperature or degree days, runoff and crop yields. There are many examples that I could have presented, but the following may suffice for the main purpose I have in mind. That purpose is to demonstrate the validity of the view that weather and crop records are not necessarily random numbers just because they may look like random numbers, and that their repetitive characteristic, if recognized, has practical value for government and business and may serve to stimulate research into the causes of the variety of repetitions.

The examples are drawn from the following nine records:

1. Annual Rainfall, Washington, D.C.
2. Annual Rainfall, Baltimore, Md.
3. Annual Rainfall, Paris, France
4. Seasonal Degree Heating Days (temperature), Baltimore, Md.
5. July Rainfall, Fifth Crop Reporting District, Iowa
6. Annual Corn Yields, Illinois
7. Annual Cotton Yields, U.S.
8. Annual Runoff, Sioux City, Iowa
9. Maximum Discharge, the Dalles, Washington

Some of them illustrate forecasts made and tested. Some indicate what forecasts could have been made. Some show the existence of patterns of fluctuations that repeat for a few years and give way to others, and some show repetitions that prevail for as many as ten to twenty years.

Chart 23. *Four Series of Annual Rainfall in Paris, 1929-1933, 1939-1943, 1949-1953, 1959-1963 and their Forecasting Series*

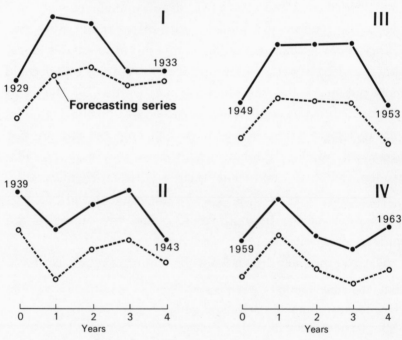

In every one of these nine cases only the simplest method of plain graphic correlation has been used; the relationships between the independent and the dependent, or repeating,

168

series is so obvious that there is no need at this stage for computing coefficients of correlation or other statistical measures of relationship.

Annual Rainfall—Washington, Baltimore, Philadelphia and Paris

The simplest of these four cases of repetition in annual rainfall is the one for Paris, France. In Chart 23 the annual variations are given for four periods: 1929-33, 1939-43, 1949-53 and 1959-63. The first point to note is that the four patterns are ten years apart. The second point is that the four patterns are not alike, except for the fact that the 1959-63 pattern is just the opposite of the 1939-43 pattern.

Below each of these patterns in Chart 23 there is another pattern, shown in dotted line. These four patterns are also dissimilar. We now have four different sets of two patterns each, and in each set the two patterns are highly correlated. The dotted series in each set is nothing more than the four symmetrically preceding yearly figures. This is a case of four different patterns repeating similar preceding patterns at a fixed interval.

Perhaps the most interesting fact about this analysis is that the fourth set represents an actual test in forecasting. Having observed in the record of more than 100 years that repetitions tend to occur at intervals of ten years, I submitted a forecasting pattern to be expected for the five years after 1959 to the Chief of the U.S. Weather Bureau. When the actual data for the years 1960-64 became available, the forecasting series turned out to have been an excellent basis for the five-year forecast, as may be seen in Table 19.

Table 19. Five-Year Forecast of Annual Rainfall, Paris, 1960-1964

	Forecasts*	Actual
1960	780	760
1961	600	563
1962	500	504
1963	600	613
1964	420	540

For series ending with 1959

The differences are amazingly small for the first four years, and even the fifth gave a useful indication of the direction of change.

The second illustration, in Chart 24, deals with another case of a tested series of forecasts. For Washington, D.C., at the end of 1956, I had identified the pattern that had been repeated for the years 1950-56 and in this case, too, submitted forecasts to the Chief of the Weather Bureau, which were subsequently borne out, as shown by the dotted line of *Forecasts* after 1956.

The actual record of annual rainfall fluctuation for the fourteen years 1950-64 is shown in the upper part of Chart 24. The lower section contains the similar data for the symmetrically preceding fluctuations. Through each of the two series I have drawn trend lines that pass approximately through the midpoints of the fluctuations. Note how accurately the fluctuations around the trend of the pre-1950 forecasting series match the fluctuations of the 1950-64 series around its trend. When this analysis is applied to the years 1965-68, it shows that these four years were also accurately predicted—a case of repetition over a span of eighteen years.

The Philadelphia illustration covers the ten-year period of annual rainfall for the years 1956-65. The years 1964 and 1965 marked an unusual dry period throughout the North-

*Chart 24. Annual Rainfall, Washington, D.C., 1950-1964,
a Forecasting Series, and Forecasts for 1957-1964*

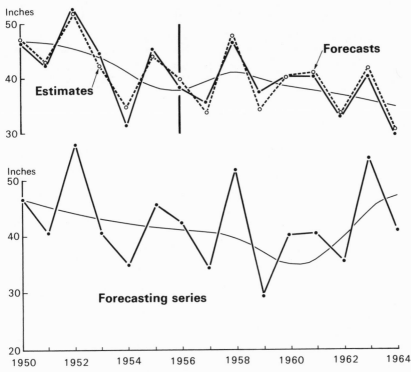

east and no one, so far as I know, was able to predict when the drought would end. Examining the long-term record of annual rainfall for Philadelphia covering more than 100 years, I was able to identify the pattern of fluctuations that the 1950-56 fluctuation appeared to be repeating. The earlier pattern is indicated by the dotted line in the upper section of Chart 25 (which appeared in the September 1966 issue of *Cycles*, the official Bulletin of the Foundation for the Study of Cycles). It pointed to an increase in rainfall for 1966 and 1967, and therefore to the end of the drought period. In 1966 the rainfall total amounted to forty inches and in 1967 to forty-four inches, practically as predicted.

171

*Chart 25.   Annual   Rainfall,   Philadelphia,   Pa.,   1956-1965
and Forecasts for 1966 and 1967; Five-year Aver-
ages of Rainfall, Baltimore, Md., and Forecasts
for 1966-1970 and 1971-1975*

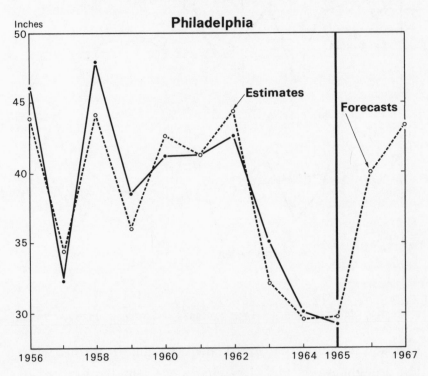

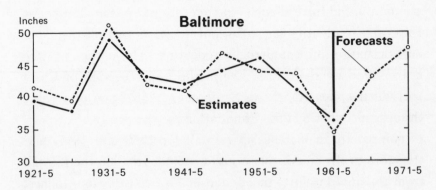

For Baltimore, Maryland, the lower section of Chart 25 contains five-year averages of rainfall for the forty-five-year span 1921 - 65. The dotted line is the record of five-year averages for an earlier fifty-five-year period. The actual averages for the 1921 - 65 period, nine in number, repeated fairly closely the averages of the earlier period. If this correlation prevails, the average for 1967 - 70 should show a gain over the drought average of 1961 - 65, and the 1971 - 75 average should show a further increase.

July Rainfall, Fifth Crop Reporting District, Iowa

The Fifth Crop Reporting District of Iowa embraces a group of counties in the central part of the state. For this district the variations in July rainfall departures from the normal are given in Chart 26 for the fourteen-year period 1943 - 56, together with estimates for the first half of the period and forecasts for the second half. The graphic method of deriving the estimates and forecasts differs slightly from the method employed for Washington, D.C., rainfall in Chart 24. Instead of measuring departures from the trend lines of the "current" and earlier series, I here resorted to graphic devices for determining a trend common to both the 1943 - 56 period and the earlier segments of the record. The procedure is this: The earlier part of the record, indicated by the hollow dots, is plotted inversely and the trend line is drawn approximately halfway between these inverted figures and their corresponding figures in the 1943 - 56 segment. In this way we avoid the use of two trends. The estimates and the forecasts are then obtained by plotting the positive deviations of the inverted series from the common trend as negative deviations from the common trend. Similarly, negative deviations of the inverted series from the common trend are plotted as positive deviations from the common trend.

Chart 26. Rainfall Departures, 5th Crop Reporting District, Iowa, 1943 - 1956, a Forecasting Series, and Forecasts for 1951 - 1956

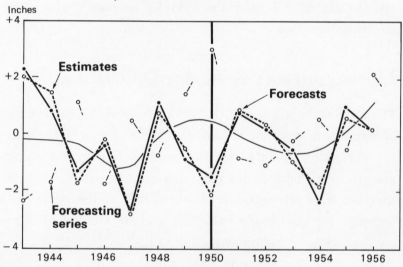

The estimates and forecasts obtained by this simplified method of graphic correlation very closely reproduce the actual variations. This is a case of a long sequence of thirteen points correctly and closely repeating a similar, earlier sequence when trend is taken into account.

Seasonal Heating Degree Days, Baltimore

Temperature records as well as rainfall records lend themselves to forecasting on the basis of repetitions. To illustrate this, Chart 27 presents the seasonal temperature degree days

174

for Baltimore for two twelve-year periods, 1920 - 32 and 1936 - 48, together with estimates for part of each series and forecasts for the remaining years. By using the graphic method for determining common trends (as described on pp. 173 - 74),

Chart 27. *Seasonal Heating Degree Days, Baltimore, Md., 1920 - 1932 and 1936 - 1948, and Forecasts for 1928 - 1932 and 1946 - 1948*

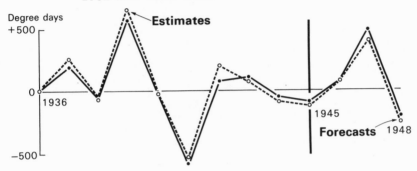

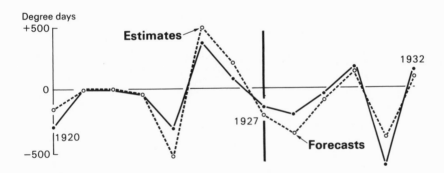

it was possible to obtain close estimates of the variations in degree days for the years 1920 - 27 and forecasts for the next five years, 1928 - 32. Similarly, it was possible to obtain the exceedingly close estimates for the years 1936 - 45 and forecasts for the next three years. "Estimates" indicate the reconstructions based on the relationships established for the

175

periods of analysis (1936-45 and 1920-27) whereas "Forecasts" indicate results obtained by applying these relationships to the subsequent years (1946-48 and 1928-32).

Chart 28. Annual Runoff at Sioux City, Iowa, 1937-1951, a Forecasting Series, and Forecasts for 1950 and 1951

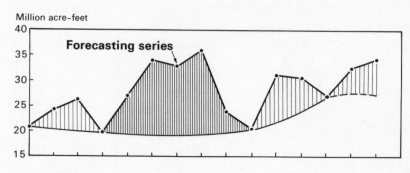

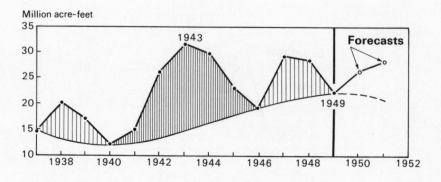

Annual Runoff, Sioux City, Iowa

The record of the annual amount of water that flows down the Missouri River at Sioux City, Iowa, is officially considered as a series of random numbers. Two segments of that record are shown in Chart 28. The first is for the period 1902-

176

16, the second for 1937-49. By connecting the low points of each record we see three cyclical episodes in each series, three-year cycles in each case separated by a six-year cycle. The correspondence between the cyclical components of the two series is striking. On the assumption that the runoff for 1950-51 and 1951-52 would continue to repeat the earlier section of the record, I gave officials of the U.S. Department of Agriculture a warning that for the 1951-52 season Sioux City would experience flood trouble, since the earlier pattern pointed to a rise in runoff above the 1949 figure and a further rise in 1951-52, to a flood level. Sioux City was flooded in the 1951-52 season. This analysis also provided a correct indication of a sharp falling off in runoff in 1953 and 1954.

It should be added that between these two segments of the runoff record shown in Chart 28 we could show two additional ones, one of them also a repetition of the other. Each of the two segments not shown here also contains three cyclical components, but the middle one in each segment is a five-year instead of a six-year cycle.

Maximum Discharge of the Columbia River at the Dalles

It is generally known that the flow of the Columbia River at the Dalles reaches a peak, or maximum, during one day in early summer, and the magnitude of that day's flow can be traced to the amount of winter snow and spring rainfall and temperature. But these causal weather factors are not meteorologically predictable a year in advance. The record of maximums is officially considered to be a random series.

For the years 1938-48 the record appears in Chart 29. In

177

*Chart 29.   Maximum Discharge of Columbia River at The
Dalles, 1938-1951, a Forecasting Series, and Forecasts for 1949-1951*

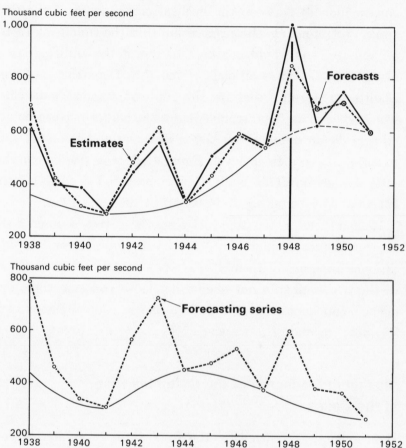

the lower section of the chart is a segment of the record for
a preceding period. For the purposes of this analysis, the annual variations in each segment are shown to deviate from
the underlying trends which connect their low points. When
the deviations from the trend in the lower segment are plotted as deviations from the trend in the upper segment, we can

178

see how closely the variations from 1938 to 1948 repeated the earlier variations.

One of the interesting features of this analysis is the estimate of the high flood point of 1948. Had this fact of repetition been known in 1947, the late industrialist Henry Kaiser and the industrial community of Vanport would have had ample advance warning of the 1948 flood and sixteen lives might have been saved. Another feature is the fact that by projecting the 1937 - 48 trend it was possible to make the actual accurate forecasts for the three years 1949 - 51, submitted in advance each year to Dr. Walter Langbein of the U.S. Geologic Survey.

The Yield Per Acre of Corn and Cotton

The two final illustrations, showing repetitive patterns in corn and cotton, are drawn from a fairly large number of similar studies of annual variations in crop yields for various crops for the U.S. as a whole, for states and counties, and for crops in a number of other countries.

Chart 30 is a simple presentation of the actual yields of corn for the state of Illinois for four seven-year periods, beginning with 1929, 1939, 1949 and 1959. Lines connecting the low yields of the second and sixth years of each period show that the deviations above them appear to have a common cyclical five-year pattern. While the patterns are not exactly alike, they appear to be sufficiently similar to provide a basis for forecasting. If this pattern repeats again after 1969, farmers in Illinois can expect higher yields in 1971 and 1972 than in 1970 and 1974, with a fair chance of an increase in 1975.

*Chart 30.   Yield Per Acre of Corn in Illinois for Four 6-year
             Periods, 1929-1935, 1939-1945, 1949-1955 and
             1959-1965*

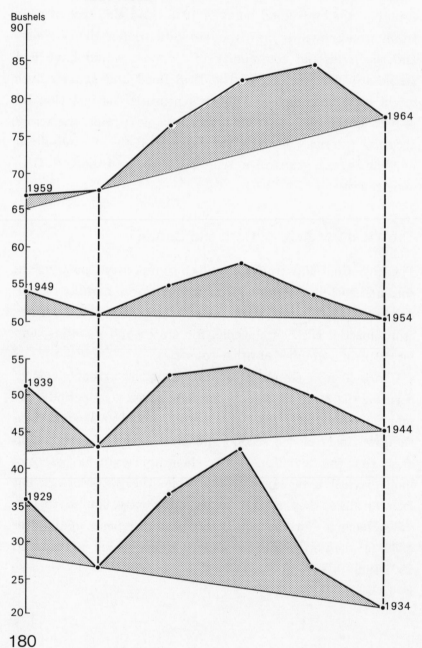

180

Chart 31 contains an analysis and a series of forecasts that I find unusually impressive. It shows that for a period of twenty years the fluctuations in the yield per acre of cotton in the United States have duplicated the fluctuations of previous years. (In fact, this series of repetitions starts with 1924.) The yield variations for the period 1927-36 I found to be inversely correlated with the yields a decade earlier. This fact I first observed in 1936 and used in December 1936 as the basis for forecasting a record yield for 1937 and subsequent record yields for 1942, 1944, 1953 and 1958. These forecasts, as well as those for the intervening years, were made available in advance to officials of the U.S. Department of Agriculture. As in other illustrations, the estimates for 1927-36 and the actual forecasts for the years 1937-47, shown in Chart 31, were obtained by plotting the negative deviations from the common trend as positive deviations. In actual practice, as in other illustrations where the common trend contains a degree of cyclicality, the trend, of course, needs to be projected with some degree of judgment when a forecast is made a year or more in advance. With only slight modification this sequence of repetition in yearly changes held good for the entire forty-two-year period from 1927 to 1969. In view of the shifts in areas of production this case of repetition is most striking.

In the foregoing illustrations there are, in all, eleven cases of repetitions; four of them repetitions of fluctuations of eleven to thirteen years; three of repetitions lasting fourteen to seventeen years; and two lasting twenty-three and twenty-four years. It may be argued that by going through several pages of random numbers it might be possible to find cases where ten, fifteen or twenty consecutive numbers are followed respectively by ten, fifteen or twenty numbers of the same magni-

181

tudes arranged in the same order. What are the chances of being able to find such repetitions in random numbers? Or, asking the question in another way, what are your chances in a game of coin tossing if you offer to match every head or tail that comes up in ten, fifteen or twenty consecutive tosses? You could expect to match ten tosses in a row once in 1,024 tries, fifteen tosses in a row once in 32,768 tries, and twenty tosses in a row once in 1,048,576 tries.

Chart 31.   Yield Per Acre of Cotton, U.S., 1927 - 1946, a Forecasting Series, and Forecasts for 1937 - 1946

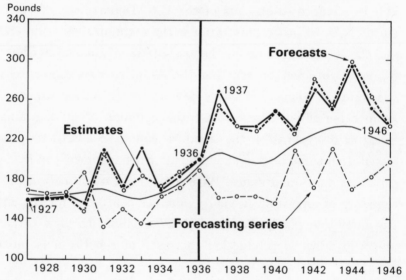

Undoubtedly, tests, other than the simple coin-tossing test, of randomness need to be applied, since in these and many other weather and crop illustrations there are factors to be taken into account, namely, changing trends and changing lags and periodicities. But even this simple test applied to examples presented here is sufficient for the conclusion that in weather and crop data there is more orderliness and year-to-year predictability than is generally recognized.

The foregoing illustrations are only a small part of the evidence I have accumulated of the possibilities in long-range weather and crop forecasting. Their practical value is obvious. Farmers everywhere, agriculturally based industries, power plants, land, sea and air transport systems, all in their various interests and problems face the uncertainties and mysteries of weather next year and beyond. The science of meteorology does not yet bridge the weather forces of this week or month to those of next year and beyond. It has been said that those who claim that they can predict weather more than a few days ahead are charlatans. I do not, of course, aspire to be put into that category, but I do hope that the illustrations I have presented will stimulate others to take the unmistakable evidences of long-range repetitions seriously enough to search for their causes.

Bibliography

PART I

Alexander, Sidney S. "Rate of Change Approaches to Forecasting—Diffusion Indexes and First Differences," *The Economic Journal,* June 1958.

Bassie, V. *Economic Forecasting.* New York: McGraw-Hill Book Co., 1958.

Bean, Louis H. "Steel Required for Full Employment," Washington, D.C., *Subcommittee of the Senate to Study Problems of American Small Business, June 19, 1947.*

Bean, Louis H., P. H. Bollinger, and O. V. Wells, *Non-Agricultural Income As a Measure of Domestic Demand,* U.S. Department of Agriculture, 1937.

Broida, A. L. "Diffusion Indexes," *American Statistician,* June 1955.

Burns, A. F., and W. C. Mitchell. *Measuring Business Cycles.* New York: National Bureau of Economic Research, Inc., 1946.

Butler, W. F., and R. A. Kavesh. *How Business Economists Forecast.* New York: Prentice-Hall, Inc., 1967.

Colm, G., and T. Geyer. *The Economy of the American People.* Washington, D.C.: National Planning Association, 1967.

Council of Economic Advisors, *The Economic Report of the President,* Washington, D.C., 1967.

Fiedler, E. R. "Long-lead and Short-lead Indexes of Business Indicators," *The American Statistical Association Proceedings of the Business and Economic Section,* 1962.

Gordan, R. A. "Alternative Approaches to Forecasting: The Recent Work of the National Bureau," *The Review of Economics and Statistics,* March 1962.

Harvard University, Review of Economics and Statistics. "Review for the Year 1928," January 1929.

———. C. J. Bullock and W. L. Crum, "The Harvard Index of Economic Conditions; Interpretation and Performance, 1919-1932," June 1932.

Karsten, Karl. "The Harvard Business Indexes—A New Interpretation," *Journal of the American Statistical Association,* December 1926.

McKinley, D. H. "Forecasting Business Conditions," The American Bankers Association, 1965.

Mitchell, W. C. *Business Cycles, the Problem and Its Setting.* New York: National Bureau of Economic Research, 1927.

Moore, G. *Business Cycle Indicators,* National Bureau of Economic Research, 1961.

Moore, G., and J. Shiskin. *Indicators of Business Expansion and Contraction,* The National Bureau of Economic Research, 1967.

Okum, A. M. "On the Appraisal of Cyclical Turning Point Indicators, *Journal of Business,* April 1960.

Shiskin, J. *Signals of Recession and Recovery,* Occasional Paper 77, New York: National Bureau of Economic Research, 1961.

U.S. Department of Commerce. *Business Cycle Developments,* Monthly Reports of the Bureau of the Census.

————. *U.S. Economic Growth to 1975—Potentials and Problems,* December 1966.

PART II

Banks, J. E. *Selected Stock Market Indicators and Their Current Implications,* 1957 Proceedings of the Business and Economic Statistics Section, American Statistical Association.

Bean, L. H. *How to Predict the Stock Market.* Washington, D.C.: Robert Luce, Inc., 1962.

Bernhard, Arnold. *The Evaluation of Common Stocks.* New York: Simon and Schuster, 1959.

Bishop, G. W. *Charles H. Dow and the Dow Theory.* New York: Appleton-Century-Crofts, Inc., 1960.

Farrell, Maurice, L. *The Dow Jones Investors Handbook.* Princeton, N.J.: Dow Jones Books, 1967.

Gerard, Karen N. "Forecasting the Stock Market" in W. F. Butler and R. A. Kavesh, (eds.), *How Business Economists Forecast.* Englewood Cliffs, N.J.: Prentice-Hall, Inc., 1966.

Graham, Benjamin. *Security Analysis: Principles and Technique.* New York: McGraw-Hill, Inc., 1962.

Molodovsky, N. "Stock Values and Stock Prices," *Financial Analysts Journal,* May 1960, March 1961, and March 1963.

PART III

Bean, Louis H. *Ballot Behavior; a Study of Presidential Elections.* Washington, D.C.: Public Affairs Press, 1940.

————. "Democratic Victory Seen—Midterm Spell May Be Broken," *Washington Post,* January 19, 1962.

———. "Election Prospects for 1960," *The New Republic,* January - July, 1960.

———. *Forecasting the California Election: The Meaning of the 1958 Primaries.* Washington, D.C.: Public Affairs Press, 1958.

———. *How to Predict Elections.* New York: Alfred A. Knopf, 1948.

———. *Influences in the 1954 Mid-Term Election: War, Jobs, Parity, McCarthy.* Washington, D.C.: Public Affairs Institute, 1954.

———. "Lessons in Political Forecasting for 1964," *American Statistical Association,* New York Chapter, April 1964.

———. *The Mid-Term Battle.* Washington, D.C.: Cantillon Books, 1950.

———. *The 1964 Presidential Election Game.* Vienna, Va.: Fairfax Publishing Co., 1964.

———. "Tides and Patterns in American Politics," *The American Political Science Review,* August 1942.

———. "Why Kennedy Won," *The Nation,* November 26, 1960.

Bean, Louis H., and Roscoe Drummond. "L. B. J. and the Elections: Trouble Ahead," *Look Magazine,* October 5, 1966.

———. "How Many Votes Does Goldwater Own?" *Look Magazine,* March 23, 1965.

Petersen, Svend. *American Presidential Elections.* New York: Frederick Ungar Publishing Co., 1963.

Scammon, R. M. *America Votes: A Handbook of Contemporary American Election Statistics.* Vols. 1 - 6. Washington, D.C.: Governmental Affairs Institute, 1964.

———. *America at the Polls: Handbook of American Presidential Elections.* Washington, D.C.: Governmental Affairs Institute, 1965.

White, T. H. *The Making of the President, 1960.* New York: Atheneum, 1961.

———. *The Making of the President, 1964.* New York: Atheneum, 1965.

U.S. Department of Commerce, Bureau of the Census. *Statistical Abstract,* 1966.

PART IV

Bean, Louis H. "Crop Yields and Weather," U.S. Department of Agriculture, Miscellaneous Bulletin 471, February 1942.

———. "Fluctuations in Crops and Weather, 1866 - 1948," Statistical Bulletin 101, U.S. Department of Agriculture, June 1951.

———. "Forecasts of Annual Rainfall for Philadelphia and Baltimore" in *Cycles: Bulletin of the Foundation for the Study of Cycles,* September 1966, p. 208; November 1966, p. 259.

————. "The Predictability of Cycles, Trends and Annual Fluctuations in Weather and Crops" in C.A.E.D. Report 20, *Weather and Our Food Supply,* The Center for Agricultural and Economic Development, Iowa State University, Ames, Iowa, 1964.

————. "The Predictability of Long-range Fluctuations in Crops and Weather" (unpublished), Discussion at Secretary's Staff Meeting, June 20, 1952, U.S. Department of Agriculture.

————. "Predicting Next Year's Weather and Crops, Statistically," paper presented at annual meeting of the American Geophysical Union, Washington, D.C., April 20, 1967.

Mitchell, J. Murray, Jr. "A Critical Appraisal of Periodicities in Climate" in C.A.E.D. Report 20, The Center for Agricultural and Economic Development, Iowa State University, Ames, Iowa, 1964.

Namias, Jerome. "Nature and Possible Causes of the Northeastern United States Drought During 1962-1965," *Monthly Weather Review,* Vol. 94, September 1966, pp. 543-54.

Palmer, Wayne C. "Meteorological Drought," Research Paper No. 45, U.S. Weather Bureau, Washington D.C., 1965.

Stallings, James L. "A Measure of Influence of Weather and Crop Production," *Journal of Farm Economics,* Vol. 43, pp. 1153-1159, 1961.

Thompson, Louis M. "Evaluation of Weather Factors in the Production of Grain Sorghums," *Agronomy Journal,* Vol. 52, pp. 182-85, 1963.

————. "Evaluation of Weather Factors in the Production of Wheat," *Journal of Soil and Water Conservation,* Vol. 17, p. 149, 1962.

————. "Weather and Technology in the Production of Corn and Soybeans" in C.A.E.D. Report 17, The Center for Agricultural and Economic Development, Iowa State University, Ames, Iowa, 1963.

————. "Weather Influences on Corn Yields," Proceedings of Agricultural Research Institute, National Academy of Science, Washington, D.C., 1964.

Wallace, Henry A. "Mathematical Inquiry into the Effect of Weather on Corn Yield in the Eight Corn Belt States," *Monthly Weather Review,* Vol. 48, pp. 439-56, 1920.

Index

191

194

About the Author

LOUIS H. BEAN was formerly Chief Economist of the Department of Agriculture and has an outstanding reputation in the business and economic world as a forecaster. He has written several books on forecasting the stock market and elections and was the only reputable man in the forecasting business to predict Truman's election in 1948. Born in Lithuania, he received his B.A. from the University of Rochester and his M.B.A. from the Harvard School of Business. He lives with his wife in Arlington, Virginia.